愛之初體驗

Journey to Home

李穎蕾 Santayana Li

香港藝術節委約及製作
Commissioned & produced by
the Hong Kong Arts Festival

英文翻譯　張菁
English Translation　Gigi Chang

With thanks to Kevin Bartholomew, Mikel Echeverría, Siân Rees and
Nathan Wisniewski for proofreading and suggestions.

Foreword

As with the child, when a play leaves the playwright's hands, many people get involved to guide its progress. A production team puts the work on stage in front of an audience, who then co-create the living experience of theatre in performance. This is the first step in the life of a new play.

Many people are needed again for the next step. The Hong Kong Arts Festival (HKAF) New Play Selection in book and e-book form, aims to facilitate the journey beyond a HKAF premiere season to subsequent stagings, new productions and new audiences.

I thank my colleagues who continue to inspire me with their dedication. With the team, I thank all the artists and co-creators who make the HKAF a living reality. It is a mark of Hong Kong's sophistication and maturity in theatre making that the new plays presented in the HKAF are warmly anticipated by an audience ready to participate in the co-creation. I look forward to journey towards higher trajectories in the years beyond the 40th HKAF.

Tisa Ho
Executive Director, Hong Kong Arts Festival

前言

劇作跟孩子的成長歷程類同,當一部劇作脫離編劇之手,許多人會參與舞台劇的製作過程,而在現場表演的一刻,觀衆其實也一起共同創作活現在舞台上戲劇的真實體驗。這就是新劇開展生命的第一步。

下一步需要更多人的參與,香港藝術節《新劇本選》的實體書及電子書系列將新劇作品在藝術節首演後推廣到更多舞台、新的製作團隊和新的觀衆群中。

我要感謝我的同事,他們全情投入的熱誠不斷為我帶來新靈感。我和我的團隊要感謝所有參演的藝術家及共同創作者,香港藝術節因有了你們才能如此生動真實。觀衆對香港藝術節呈獻的新劇報以熱切期待,並積極參與,這標誌着香港戲劇已邁向細緻和成熟的階段。我期待香港戲劇在第 40 屆香港藝術節往後的年月中能躍升至更高平台。

何嘉坤
香港藝術節行政總監

Playwright's Notes

I presented my very first play on 12 April 2010. When I tried to introduce the play to my teachers and schoolmates, I was so agitated that I could not speak and tears streamed uninterrupted. I realised it takes immense courage and genuine openness to lay bare my innermost world for others.

I would like to thank a Cantonese opera artist, I found the inspiration to muster my courage. When he practices calligraphy, he holds the ink brush in his right hand and a cigarette in his left. With each puff, the smoke he exhales cuts like the swish of a sword – palpable, all-penetrating and refreshing. His chivalry and righteousness has awakened many slumbering souls, introducing them to the grand world of theatre. I'd like to say to him: "Your smoke has changed my life."

Another inspiration is also a keen smoker. He is a police officer. Every day, he carries a .38 revolver to protect his loved ones. He never shied away from performing his duty or fulfilling his role in life. From the day I was born, I came under the protection of his .38 revolver. Now that he has retired, the revolver is replaced by a content smile, which reassures me on a daily basis. "Thank you, my dear old man. You led me to adulthood, and you brought me up to become someone who loves to laugh."

The last one is a woman of mystery. My creative motivation originates from her. In some ways, she is the one who takes me to another realm, to a world which I have never been. I want to tell her, "Your love for me is sufficed in its subtleness. Anything too overt would not be your style. I got my dry and scaly hands from you. Others may not like it, but I don't care, because these hands are the embodiment of love. Thank you."

編者的話

2010 年 4 月 12 日，我將我第一次寫的劇本於校內發表，當時我向老師和同學們介紹這齣戲時，激動得說不出話來，眼淚也不停地流。我發現，要和別人分享自己內心世界，需要莫大的勇氣、赤裸地表露和真誠的心意。

我之所以能夠鼓起莫大的勇氣，全因為得到一位文武生的啟發。當他的右手拿着毛筆寫大字時，左手則拿着香煙在抽。每抽一下，呼出來的煙就像看得到的劍氣般穿透、振奮人心。他那種行俠仗義的劍道精神，喚醒了不少沉睡的靈魂，將他們帶入劇場的後花園。我跟他說：「你的煙，改變了我的人生。」

另外一位啟蒙者也是一個愛抽煙的人，他是一名警察，每天陀着一支點 38 的左輪手槍來保護自己深愛的人。他從來都不吝嗇向別人表露他的身份和責任。從我出生至今，我就是被他的點 38 手槍保護着。現在他已經退休了，他把他的手槍化成笑容，每天向我報以一個滿足的微笑。「感謝你，可愛的老頭，不但將我撫養成人，也令我成為一個愛笑的人。」

最後一位是一個深不可測的女人。我創作的動力也是來自她。某程度來說是她帶我去另一個領域，一個我從來沒有去過的國度。我想跟她說：「你對我的愛，淡淡的已經足夠，太濃就不像是你的作風。我又乾又皺的手是遺傳自你的，別人會不喜歡但我就是不管，因為這雙手是愛的憑據。謝謝你。」

For the unassuming Michael, I like how you use a music stand and conduct music that moves hearts (mine at least). Believe me, you are much better than Karajan.

I am grateful to the Hong Kong Arts Festival for taking good care of me. Thank you, Mr Poon Wai-sum, Mr Lee Chun-chow, Mr So Kwok-wan, Ian, Kathy, Yuen, Gigi and Alexia.

Also I'd like to thank the actors and the backstage crew. You are the cradle of the play and you give it life.

This play is more than a semi-autobiographical sketch, it is a living story about my family.

Finally, my thanks to each and everyone one of you in the audience, for walking with me on this *journey to home*.

Thank you!

Santayana Li
李穎蕾

Li graduated from the School of Drama of the Hong Kong Academy for Performing Arts (HKAPA) in 2011, where she received the Cheung Tat-ming Playwright Scholarship. As a performer, her recent productions include *Moses in Love* (BHT Theatre), *Cricket in My Life* (third run, Prospects Theatre), *The House of Bernarda Alba* (Seals Players Foundation) and *Gao Xingjian's Of Mountains and Seas* (world premiere, Chinese University of Hong Kong's Hong Kong Drama Programme). Her first two plays, *Journey to Home* and *Part Timer*, were presented at the Prospects Theatre's Playwright Scheme V and VI in 2010 and 2011 respectively. In February 2012, Li will return to the HKAPA for a Master of Fine Arts in Drama, specialising in playwriting.

低調的 Michael，很喜歡你用譜架，指揮出動人（至少動我）心弦的樂章。相信我，你比 Karajan 勁好多。

感謝香港藝術節對我的愛護。感謝潘惠森先生、李鎮洲先生、蘇國雲先生、Ian、Kathy、Yuen、Gigi、Alexia。

還有一眾演員和後台工作人員，你們令劇本有生命、有機的盛載着。

這不是一個只寫給我的半自傳式故事，而是一個寫給我的家有血有肉的故事。

感謝每一位入場的觀眾與我一同經歷一次深刻的人生旅程。

多謝！

2011 年畢業於香港演藝學院戲劇學院（榮譽）學士學位，主修表演。在校期間曾獲張達明劇作獎學金。最近演出有 BHT 劇團《情場摩西》及新域劇團《三姊妹與哥哥和一隻蟋蟀》（三度公演）。其他演出作品包括：海豹劇團三十周年《深閨大宅》、香港中文大學戲劇工程 — 世界首演高行健《山海經傳》等。創作方面，兩度（2010-11）參加新域劇團《劇場裡的虎與藏龍》V 及 VI，編寫人生第一個作品《愛之初體驗》及第二個作品《Part Timer》。今年 2 月於香港演藝學院攻讀研究生課程，主修編劇。

《愛之初體驗》首演於第 40 屆香港藝術節，
2012 年 2 月 10 日，香港文化中心劇場

Journey to Home premiered at the 40th Hong Kong Arts
Festival, Studio Theatre, Hong Kong Cultural Centre,
10 February 2012

監製 Producer
香港藝術節 Hong Kong Arts Festival

編劇 Playwright
李穎蕾 Santayana Li

導演 Director
李鎮洲 Lee Chun-chow

佈景設計 Set Designer
小蕉（邵偉敏）Siujiou (Siu Wan-man)

服裝及造型設計 Costume & Image Designer
何珮姍 Ho Pui-shan, Cindy

燈光設計 Lighting Designer
楊子欣 Yeung Tsz-yan

音樂及音響設計 Music and Sound Designer
彭俊傑 Pang Chun-kit

製作經理 Production Manager
張向明 Cheung Heung-ming

主演 Cast

少女	楊淇
Girl	Kate Yeung
女人	伍潔茵
Woman	Ng Kit-yan, Cecilia
女子	郭翠怡
Young Women	Kwok Chui-yi
男人	陳永泉
Man	Chan Wing-chuen
少男	阮少泓
Boy	Juan Shao-hong

Scenes

Scene 1   Taiwan home

Scene 2   Hong Kong home

Scene 3   Taiwan home

Scene 4   A cafe in Ximending, Taiwan

Scene 5   A park in Central, Hong Kong

Scene 6   Taiwan home

Scene 7   Yangmingshan, night

Scene 8   Taiwan home

Scene 9   Hong Kong home

Scene 10   A cafe in Ximending, Taiwan

Scene 11   Hong Kong home

Scene 12   Tamsui, Taiwan

Scene 13   A classic outdoor cafe in Central, Hong Kong

Scene 14   An open ground in Taipei

Scene 15   On the ferry

Scene 16   Hong Kong home

Scene 17   Home

分場表

第一場	台灣家
第二場	香港家
第三場	台灣家
第四場	台灣西門町的一間 cafe
第五場	香港中環的一個公園
第六場	台灣家
第七場	陽明山夜景
第八場	台灣家
第九場	香港家
第十場	台灣西門町的一間 cafe
第十一場	香港家
第十二場	台灣淡水
第十三場	香港中環的一個舊式露天茶檔
第十四場	台北市的一個空地
第十五場	離島船上
第十六場	香港家
第十七場	家

Scene
台灣家
Taiwan home

Scene 1 Taiwan home

Lights up.

A WOMAN and a GIRL staring at each other.

The WOMAN is wearing one high heel shoe, the other one is in her hand. The GIRL stands outside the front door. She is dressed in a t-shirt and shorts, with a backpack on her back and a carrier bag in her hand.

The door is wide open.

A long silence.

Woman: *(Smiles)* You've come?

The GIRL stares at the WOMAN.

Silence.

The GIRL walks inside the flat, finds a spot to stand and resumes staring at the WOMAN.

Silence.

Girl: Didn't you say you were going to pick me up?

Woman: I'm putting my shoes on... *(Smiles)* A bit late.

Silence.

Woman: I'm so happy you're here. *(Reaches for the carrier bag)* Give it to me, I'll take it into your room.

The WOMAN heads toward the room, stops, and takes off her shoe. She turns around to look at the GIRL, who has not moved at all.

Woman: Do sit. *(Disappears into the room)*

The GIRL remains standing. She notices a small greasy paper bag on the coffee table.

The WOMAN returns, still holding the shoes she was wearing earlier.

第一場　台灣家

　　　　　　燈亮

　　　　　　【一個女人和一個少女對望着】

　　　　　　【女人一隻腳穿了高跟鞋，另一隻高跟鞋在她一邊手上；少女站在大門外，身穿 T-shirt 短褲、揹着一個背包和一個手提袋】

　　　　　　【大門開着】

　　　　　　【長久靜默】

女人：　　（笑）你嚟咗？

　　　　　　【少女望着女人】

　　　　　　【靜默】

　　　　　　【少女走入屋，站在一個位置，然後繼續望着女人】

　　　　　　【靜默】

少女：　　你唔係話嚟接我架咩？

女人：　　我着緊鞋架⋯⋯（笑）係遲咗啲。

　　　　　　【靜默】

女人：　　你嚟咗我就開心。（笑着拿少女手上的手提袋）俾我，我幫你拎入房。

　　　　　　【女人走入房途中停下，脫下鞋子，然後轉身望向正站立的少女】

女人：　　坐啦。（入房）

　　　　　　【少女站在原地，看見茶几上有一包帶點油膩的小紙皮袋】

　　　　　　【女人走出房間，手上還是拿着剛才穿着的高跟鞋】

Woman: *(Smiles)* Try some. Bought them in Tamsui, super delicious with pickles. I get them all the time. *(Sits down on one end of the sofa)*

The GIRL stays still.

Woman: Do sit down.

The GIRL puts her backpack in the middle of the sofa and sits next to it.

A long silence.

The WOMAN puts down her shoes, picks up the remote control on the coffee table and turns on the TV. Local news is on.

The GIRL watches the news anchor with interest.

The WOMAN sits down on the other end of the sofa.

She looks at the GIRL.

Woman: How did you get here?

Girl: Bus, then taxi.

Woman: Wow, such a smart girl.

Girl: You always mention it on the phone.

Woman: Did I? I thought you were bluffing.

(Looks at the GIRL) I didn't think you'd actually come… I'm really happy you're here…

Girl : Where's Uncle?

Woman: Working in China.

Girl: When's he coming back?

Woman: He's been there for two years.

Girl: So he left right after you two got married?

女人： （笑）食吖，喺淡水度買架，加埋啲酸菜好好食，我成日都買嚟食。（走到 Sofa 一邊坐下）

【少女不動】

女人： 坐啦。

【少女將背包放在 Sofa 中間，然後坐在旁邊】

【長久靜默】

【女人放下高跟鞋，拿了茶几上的遙控器，按 Power on，電視正播着台灣本地新聞】

【少女好奇地看着電視中的新聞主播】

【女人在 Sofa 的另一邊坐下】

【女人望着少女】

女人： 係呢，你點嚟架？

少女： 搭大巴再轉的士。

女人： 哦，咁叻女識自己嚟？

少女： 你成日喺電話度教我架。

女人： 係咩？我以為你講吓咋。

（望着少女）我冇諗到你真係嚟……我好開心你嚟咗……

少女： Uncle 呢？

女人： 喺大陸做嘢。

少女： 幾時返？

女人： 佢喺嗰邊都做咗兩年……

少女： 即係你同佢一結完婚佢就走咗？

Woman: Hey!

Girl: Why didn't you move to China?

Woman: Don't like it.

Girl: You don't like him?

Woman: Why did you say that?

Girl: You're here.

Woman: What would you know?

They look at each other, speechless.

Silence.

The WOMAN goes to the kitchen.

The GIRL watches her every move.

She scans the room from the sofa. Some photographs mounted on the right side of the wall behind her catch her eye. They are of the WOMAN and different groups of foreigners. She is then drawn to the cabinet under the TV.

The noise of a blender comes from the kitchen.

The GIRL starts looking through the CDs inside the cabinet.

From the kitchen, the blender noise can be heard intermittently. The GIRL rummages through the cabinet, but can't find anything she likes. She notices the shoes by the sofa and sits back down on the same spot as before.

The WOMAN comes out with a green drink.

Woman: Try this. *(Puts the drink on the coffee table)*

Girl: I don't like this sort of thing.

女人： 喂！

少女： 你唔一齊去？

女人： 唔鍾意。

少女： 唔鍾意Uncle？

女人： 點解咁講呢？

少女： 你唔一齊去。

女人： 你識咩。

【二人對望，無言】

【靜默】

【女人入廚房】

【少女望着她入廚房】

【少女坐着，但上半身向客廳的不同方向觀察，一會，她望到她後方右側牆上，整齊地貼着多張女人與一班外國人的合照；一會，她望向電視機下的茶几】

【廚房傳出攪拌機的聲音】

【少女走到茶几面前，看裏面的 CD】

【攪拌機聲音斷斷續續出現；少女在找茶几裏的 CD】

【少女找不到她所喜歡的 CD，她轉身，看到女人的高跟鞋放在 Sofa 旁，看後她回到 Sofa 的原位坐下】

【女人從廚房出，手中拿着一杯青色的飲料】

女人： 試吓。（將青色飲料放到茶几上）

少女： 我唔鍾意飲呢啲嘢。

Woman:	It's good for you.
Girl:	I don't like it.
	Silence.
Girl:	What do you like?
Woman:	Red wine.
Girl:	Do you drink with your foreign friends?
Woman:	Yes, but they like beer. I don't. Beer belly.
	The GIRL remains seated.
	The WOMAN returns to the kitchen.
	She comes out with a glass of red wine, puts it on the table and sits down.
	Silence.
Woman:	Try this.
	The GIRL looks at it.
Woman:	When I'm out, I drink water to cleanse myself after a few glasses. But I make this (points at the green drink) when I'm home.
Girl:	I prefer water.
	Silence.
	The WOMAN goes to the kitchen.
	This time she returns with a small red carton, puts it on the table and sits down again.
Woman:	Taiwan Lemon Tea. Every boy and girl here loves it.
	The GIRL peers at the tea then at the WOMAN.
Girl:	Why won't you give me some water?

女人：　　有益架。

少女：　　我唔鍾意飲。

　　　　　【靜默】

少女：　　咁你鍾意飲咩？

女人：　　紅酒。

少女：　　同啲外國朋友飲？

女人：　　係呀，佢哋都鍾意飲啤酒。我唔鍾意，啤酒肚。

　　　　　【少女坐着】

　　　　　【女人入廚房】

　　　　　【女人拿着一杯紅酒從廚房出，將它放在茶几上，然後坐回 Sofa 上】

　　　　　【靜默】

女人：　　試吓。

　　　　　【少女望着紅酒杯】

女人：　　喺出面有時飲咗幾杯之後會飲杯水清一清，但喺屋企就會榨呢杯嘢嚟飲。

少女：　　我想飲水多啲。

　　　　　【靜默】

　　　　　【女人再入廚房】

　　　　　【女人從廚房出，拿出一盒紅色紙包飲品放在茶几上，然後坐回原位】

女人：　　「台灣檸檬茶」，係後生仔女都飲。

　　　　　【少女望着那「台灣檸檬茶」，然後望着女人】

少女：　　點解你係都唔俾水我飲呢？

Silence.

The WOMAN picks up the green drink and takes a sip.

Silence.

She then picks up the wine and downs it.

The GIRL continues to glare at the WOMAN.

The WOMAN puts on her high heels.

Woman: I'm seeing some friends. Don't wait for me.

She starts to leave, then turns around.

Woman: I'll be back soon. Bye!

She shuts the door, locks it then tries the handle a few times to make sure it is secure.

The GIRL assesses the choices of drinks. She picks the lemon tea, pulls out the straw and tastes it.

She looks around the room while she drinks. Moments later, she puts the tea down, turns off the TV and walks over to her backpack. She pulls out a DV camcorder and starts filming.

Girl: First visit… Day one… Living room...

She points her camera at one of the photographs on the wall and gives it the finger.

Girl: *(In Mandarin)* Hello!

She shoots the three sorts of drinks and the bag of stinky tofu.

Girl: Things she likes to eat and drink…

She turns off the camcorder, and starts eating and drinking.

【靜默】

【女人拿起五青汁，喝了一口，放下】

【靜默】

【女人拿起紅酒，喝光】

【少女望着女人】

【女人穿起高跟鞋】

女人：　　我約咗朋友，唔駛等我。

【女人走到門口，轉身望着少女】

女人：　　我好快返。Bye！

【女人閂門、鎖門，揸住門柄確保安全才走】

【少女望着茶几上的三種飲料，選了「台灣檸檬茶」，她抽出飲管，試喝】

【少女一邊喝一邊觀察客廳。一會，她將「台灣檸檬茶」放回茶几、關電視，然後自然地走去打開背包，拿出一部 DV 機，拍下整個空間】

少女：　　第一次……第一日……客廳……

【鏡頭走到牆上的一幅照片，少女舉起中指】

少女：　　（普通話）你好！

【鏡頭走向茶几的三款飲料和臭豆腐】

少女：　　佢鍾意食同佢鍾意飲嘅……

【少女關掉 DV 機，然後拿起「台灣檸檬茶」和臭豆腐吃】

She then pulls out her mobile phone and dials a number.

Girl: Hey, hey, it's me. I'm here… it's great, really great… All right, I'll pick something up from the Duty Free before I go… I know… OK. Bye!

She puts away the phone and reaches into her bag for a CD. She pops it into the player; a song plays quietly.

She enjoys the moment, makes herself comfortable on the floor and starts picking at the snacks again.

Lights dim. Music stops.

Lights up.

Midnight. The WOMAN returns, tipsy. She sees the GIRL sleeping on the floor and ignores her. She goes to the telephone to check for missed calls, then takes off her high heels and enters the kitchen.

She returns with a full glass of red wine and picks up the phone.

Woman: *(In Mandarin)* Hey, are you home? … I had dinner already… There's no point cooking when you're not around. *(Drinks)* You really shouldn't drink so much… I'm not like you… I do not drink. *(Chuckles)* She is really here! … My niece. Her mother died when she was little. I looked after her. Now she's all grown up, she wants to see me… I am really happy… That's correct, two of us, and happier for it! *(Laughs)* … All right, all right. Miss you. Bye!

The WOMAN stands over the sleeping GIRL with wine in hand and watches her sleep.

【少女拿出手提電話，撥號】

少女：　喂，係呀我到咗喇⋯⋯好呀，好好呀⋯⋯得喇，臨走去 Duty Free 度買俾你啦⋯⋯知道⋯⋯好啦，Bye。

【少女放下手提電話後從背包拿出一隻 CD，放入 CD 機裏面，歌曲輕聲地播着】

【少女享受着，然後放軟身子坐在地板上繼續吃】

燈暗，音樂停

燈亮

【深夜，女人帶點醉意回來，看到少女睡在地板上，她並沒有理會，走到電話旁邊看來電記錄，然後脫掉高跟鞋入廚房】

【女人拿着一隻已盛着紅酒的酒杯步出廚房，走到電話旁，拿起電話】

女人：　（普通話）喂，在家嗎？⋯⋯吃了⋯⋯你不在我一個人煮飯就沒意思了。（喝酒）你啊，不要喝那麼多！⋯⋯誰像你，我不喝酒的⋯⋯（笑）她真的來了！⋯⋯我的姪女啊，她小時候母親就死了，是我照顧她的，現在長大了就跑過來想要見我⋯⋯我很開心⋯⋯對啊，兩個人，開心就會多喝一點啊！（笑）⋯⋯好了好了，想你，Bye。

【女人拿着紅酒杯走到少女旁，看着她睡】

Woman: Silly girl, go to your room… I know you can hear me… Hey, let me teach you something. *(Places the glass of wine in front of the watch on her left wrist)* Can you see the time? Yes, then the wine is light. No? Then it's a strong one. *(Chuckles)* I only found this out today after all these years. A foreign friend taught me.

Silence.

Woman: *(Finishes the wine)* What if it's all been drunk? … There's nothing left.

Silence.

The GIRL gets up and goes to her room.

The WOMAN returns to an empty living room.

Darkness.

女人：　　傻女，返房瞓啦……我知你聽到我講嘢架。嗱，教你
　　　　　一樣嘢，（舉起戴着手錶的左手，將盛着紅酒的酒杯放
　　　　　在手表前）睇唔睇到而家幾點？睇到即係杯酒係淡嘅、
　　　　　唔太睇到呢就係濃嘅。（笑）我飲咗咁耐酒今日先知，
　　　　　係一個外國朋友教我架。

【靜默】

女人：　　（喝光紅酒）如果飲晒即係點？……飲晒囉。

【靜默】

【少女起身走入睡房】

【女人步出廚房，不見少女】

燈暗

Scene

香港家

Hong Kong home

Scene 2   Hong Kong home

Lights up.

Rear stage right, a Man in his 40s sitting on his bed. His head is resting on his right arm, his eyes closed.

Front stage left, a 22-year-old YOUNG WOMAN in uniform snacking away on crisps and Coca-Cola in front of the TV.

The MAN leaves the bedroom, lights a cigarette at front stage right.

Young
Woman: I just paid for the laundry. 48 dollars.

He smokes.

Young
Woman: The owner asked me again.

Silence.

Young
Woman: When will you pick up your clothes?

Silence.

Young   She's been our neighbour for years. That's why she
Woman: never bothered you about it. Now she's moving,
           she's gonna throw it all away.

He puffs away.

Young
Woman: You've got 'til Sunday before they get rid of everything.

Silence.

Man: When's she coming back?

Silence.

Young
Woman: Soon. Call if you're worried.

第二場　香港家

燈亮

台右後方，一位 40 多歲的男人坐在睡床上，右手枕在後腦、合上眼。

台左前方，一個 22 歲的女子穿着制服，豪邁地坐在 Sofa 上飲可樂、食薯片、睇電視。

男人步出睡房，行去台右前方，點煙。

女子：　我啱啱俾咗洗衫錢，四十八蚊。

【男人抽煙】

女子：　阿老闆娘今日又問我。

【靜默】

女子：　你幾時攞番套衫啫？

【靜默】

女子：　幾廿年街坊人哋先唔同你計咋，老闆娘要搬鋪，你再唔攞人哋掉咗佢架喇。

【男人繼續抽煙】

女子：　今個禮拜日Deadline，你唔攞人哋就掉。

【靜默】

男人：　佢幾時返？

【靜默】

女子：　差唔多啦，你擔心佢咪打個電話俾佢囉。

He keeps smoking.

Young
Woman: I won't be bothered.

He continues to smoke and she turns her attention back to the TV.

Young
Woman: She only went to Taiwan 'cause she was upset.

Silence.

Young
Woman: *(Sighs)* I want a holiday too.

Silence.

Young
Woman: What's so good about Taiwan? I don't see anything special. What's she thinking, running off like that? You won't have the money for the flight, eh? Where will you find the money?

She sits up to open another can of Coke then resumes the lounging position.

Young
Woman: She just made a lot of non-committal sounds, hmm... Erm... Hmm... Hmm... The next day all she left was a note, "I'm off to Taiwan. Don't worry. I'll bring something back." Wah, it's just a break up. I've been dumped too! Lots of times!

Silence.

Something on TV makes her laugh.

Young
Woman: That boy's still calling her. She's just not answering. I've seen that phone of hers flashing away, over and over again. 81 missed calls. I remember thinking, "Calling like there's no tomorrow... She's not stupid... She can see you've called."

Man: If it's what he wants, what's that to do with you?

【男人繼續抽煙】

女子： 我就費事打喇。

【男的繼續抽煙；女的繼續看電視】

女子： 佢唔開心先去台灣咋。

【靜默】

女子： 唉，我都想放假呀。

【靜默】

女子： 台灣好咩？我又唔覺得有咩好喎，一個人買張機票就咁走咗去想點先？你又會有錢去台灣？你邊度嚟咁多錢呀？

【女子開了另一罐可樂，攤在 Sofa 上】

女子： 佢就剩係嗯、哦、嗯、嗯，跟住第二日就咁留張紙條話：「我去台灣，放心，有手信。」嘩！失戀唔駛咁呀，我都失過唔少啦！

【靜默】

【女子睇電視，發出笑聲】

女子： 個男仔仲有打電話俾佢呀，佢唔聽咋嘛。有次我親眼見住佢個電話不停閃、閃完一次又一次，我睇住個電話有成 81 個 Miss call，我心諗：唔駛打得咁搏命呀，知架喇，見到你打嚟架喇……

男人： 人哋鍾意打咪打，關你咩事？

Silence.

Young Woman: Well… she picked up the 82nd time. Turned out to be that woman.

She joins him for a cigarette; he is still smoking.

Silence.

Young Woman: I don't really remember her. Only got this image in my head. The kitchen… She's rinsing rice… The water has turned milky… She's got a ring on her finger… And the smell of tomatoes…

Silence.

Young Woman: She beat me all the time. Left marks all over. I hate her.

Man: Did she?

Young Woman: That woman was crazy. Her nails were deadly. So sharp, they always left swollen red marks afterwards.

He grins.

Young Woman: But when she smiled at me… I like her smile.

Silence.

Young Woman: Free later?

Man: Why?

Young Woman: I want to go to Lantau.

Man: Working tonight.

Young Woman: Fuck.

Man: Your turn to buy cigarettes.

【靜默】

女子：　　咁⋯⋯個電話閃到第 82 次佢聽喇，點知係嗰個女人打嚟。

【男人繼續抽煙；女子行到旁邊一起抽煙】

【靜默】

女子：　　我對佢都冇乜印象，我剩係記得一個畫面：喺廚房⋯⋯佢洗米⋯⋯啲洗米水白矇矇⋯⋯隻手帶住隻戒指⋯⋯仲有陣蕃茄味⋯⋯

【靜默】

女子：　　佢仲成日打我添，打到我成身都係一條條痕。我憎佢。

男人：　　佢成日打你咩？

女子：　　個女人癲架，佢啲手指甲尖到死，一打落嚟成條紅色痕腫起晒！

【男人微笑】

女子：　　不過佢一對住我笑呢就⋯⋯我鍾意佢個笑容。

【靜默】

女子：　　你一陣得唔得閒？

男人：　　做咩？

女子：　　我想去大嶼山呀。

男人：　　返夜。

女子：　　妖。

男人：　　下次到你買煙。

He goes to his room. The Bee Gees's Tragedy *can be heard playing inside.*

Young
Woman:

That squealing man is awful.

She glazes over at a distant spot with the cigarette hanging off her lips. Suddenly, an overwhelming urge to sing along takes over.

Young
Woman:

Tragedy!
When the feeling's gone and you can't go on
Tragedy!
When the morning cries and you don't know why
It's hard to bear
With no one to love you, you're going nowhere
Au!

She goes to her room. The music continues.

Darkness.

【男人走回睡房。一陣，房內傳出 Bee Gees 的
《Tragedy》】

女子： 嗰條假音佬唱歌真係難聽。

【女子口含着煙，凝視着一點。突如其來的一個生理反
應，女子便跟着歌曲唱起來】

女子： *Tragedy!*
When the feeling's gone and you can't go on
Tragedy!
When the morning cries and you don't know why
It's hard to bear
With no one to love you, you're going nowhere
Au!

【女子行入睡房，音樂繼續播放着】

燈暗

Scene

台灣家

Taiwan home

Scene 3   Taiwan home

The WOMAN goes to the GIRL's room, tries the door, but it is locked.

She knocks.

No answer.

She returns to the living room and sits on the sofa.

After a moment, the door opens, the WOMAN keeps watching but no one comes out.

Woman: I'm going to school. I finish at four.

Silence.

Woman: Will you wait here?

Silence.

Woman: I've got a key and 5,000 dollars in cash on the shoe cabinet. If you need some change, it's in the glass bowl, in the living room. Be careful and don't forget the phone card. Bye!

She opens the front door and closes it, then sits back down on the sofa.

The GIRL comes out at the sound of the door shutting. She is startled to see the WOMAN.

They stare at each other.

Girl: Morning. *(Picks up the key and the money)*

Woman: Morning.

The GIRL goes back to her room.

Woman: Sleep well?

Girl: Yes.

第三場　台灣家

【女人走到少女房門口，開門，門上鎖】

【女人敲門】

【無人應門】

【女人回到客廳坐在 Sofa 上】

【一會，少女睡房門開，女人望着，但沒有人走出來】

女人：　　我而家返學，四點鐘先放。

【靜默】

女人：　　你會唔會喺屋企等我？

【靜默】

女人：　　我擺咗條鎖匙同 5000 蚊台幣喺鞋櫃頂，想要散銀就喺廳嗰個玻璃碗度擺。你自己小心啲喇，記住帶電話卡。Bye！

【女人走去大門口開門，閂門，走回去 Sofa 坐下】

【少女聽到閂門聲便從睡房門口出，之後她行出大廳，見到女人，嚇倒】

【二人對望】

少女：　　早晨。（到鞋櫃頂拿錢和鎖匙）

女人：　　早晨。

【少女走回睡房方向】

女人：　　尋晚瞓得好唔好？

少女：　　好。

Woman: You said you wanted water last night. *(Smiles)* I've bought half a dozen bottles. They're in the fridge. Help yourself.

The GIRL goes to the bathroom to get ready. The WOMAN waits on the sofa.

She comes out.

Woman: *(Smiles)* Why don't you come to school with me? The kids are really cute!

The GIRL goes to the kitchen.

She comes out with a glass of water and drinks it in the doorway.

The WOMAN looks at her.

Silence.

Girl: No.

Silence.

Woman: You're meeting someone?

Girl: No.

Woman: Where are you going then?

Girl: …

Woman: Don't you want to see how I teach the kids?

Girl: …

Woman: You can even help me.

Girl: Why would you want my help?

Silence.

Woman: I told the principal you'd come today.

The GIRL goes to her room.

女人： 你尋晚又話想飲水？（笑）我買咗半打雪咗入雪櫃，你鍾意就飲多啲。

【少女去洗手間梳洗；女人坐在 Sofa 等待】

【少女從洗手間出】

女人： （微笑）不如你跟我返學吖，啲小朋友好得意架！

【少女入廚房】

【少女拿了一杯水出，站在廚房門口旁喝水】

【女人望着少女】

【靜默】

少女： 唔去。

【靜默】

女人： 你約咗人？

少女： 冇。

女人： 咁你一陣去邊？

少女： ……

女人： 你唔想睇吓我點教啲小朋友咩？

少女： ……

女人： 你仲可以幫我手教喎。

少女： 點解要我幫你手呢？

【靜默】

女人： 我同咗個校長講話你今日會嚟。

【少女走入睡房】

Woman:	You don't have to hang around until four. Just say hi to the principal. Stay for a little while. That would do.

Phone rings. She picks up.

Woman:	Hello. Good morning Mr Chung. OK, I'll be down in five minutes. Can you wait a little longer? OK... Sorry... Bye. *(Goes to the GIRL's room)* Are you coming?

Silence.

Woman:	Just spend some time with the principal's daughter. Keep her company until she goes to her afternoon classes. Then you can go.

Silence.

Woman:	I saw her grow up. She's really cute. Well behaved and smart. I want you to meet them.

The GIRL emerges with her backpack. She is dressed and ready to go.

Girl:	Ready.

She leaves the flat.

Woman:	*(Grabs her handbag and rushes after her)* I've got a taxi downstairs.

She locks up.

Darkness.

女人：　你唔駛陪到我四點架，你同校長打個招呼、坐一陣就得架喇。

【電話響，女人接】

女人：　喂……早安鍾先生……好，我大概五分鐘到樓下……麻煩你再等一會……好……不好意思……Bye。（女人走到少女房門前）你去唔去呀？

【靜默】

女人：　同校長個女坐一陣、陪佢玩到返下晝班咁你就走得架喇！

【靜默】

女人：　佢個女我睇住佢大，好得意架佢，又乖又醒目。我都想你見吓佢哋。

【少女換好衣服、揹着背包出】

少女：　行得。

【少女開門出】

女人：　（拿手袋追）我叫咗的士喺樓下等我哋架喇。

【女人關門】

燈暗

Scene
台灣西門町的一間 cafe
A cafe in Ximending, Taiwan

Scene 4   A cafe in Ximending, Taiwan

Lights up.

A university student sitting on his own on the second floor of a cafe in Ximending. He is working on his laptop.

The GIRL enters and sits in the first empty seat she sees. She takes out a bottle of water and starts drinking.

After a few sips, she slams the bottle on the table without thinking.

The student notices her. She becomes self-conscious and puts the water away.

He nods at her; she smiles.

He returns to his work, typing away noisily.

She turns her attention to the crowd outside, trying to find a focal point amid the hustle and bustle. Failing, she stares into space.

He reaches for his coffee and notices her again.

(They converse in Mandarin unless otherwise indicated.)

Boy: Can I help?

She shakes her head.

A long silence.

Girl: I have got a family relative in Taiwan. She has been living here for almost five years. This is the first time I have come to visit her. She married a Taiwanese man three years ago. Work sent him to China soon after they got married… but she did not move with him because she does not like China. She is always very cheerful… except whenever they talk on the phone. She always asks the same questions. Are you drunk? Have you been out a lot? Have you been spending

第四場　台灣西門町的一間 cafe

燈亮

【一名大學生獨自坐在西門町的一間 cafe 二樓，他正在用手提電腦】

【少女入，見到有空位立即坐下，拿出礦泉水喝】

【喝完水之後，少女無意識地大力將水樽放在枱上】

【大學生望着少女，少女意會到他望着自己便收起礦泉水】

【大學生向少女點頭；少女微笑回應】

【大學生回到他的手提電腦，發出「撻、撻、撻、撻」的打字聲】

【少女的眼球轉移到玻璃窗外熙來攘往的人群，眼球嘗試在人群中找焦點但找不到。她發呆】

【大學生拿起他枱上的咖啡喝，他再次望到少女】

（除特別指明，以下為普通話對話）

少男：　我有什麼可以幫你嗎？

【少女搖頭】

【長久靜默】

少女：　我有一個親戚住在台灣，差不多有五年了。我是第一次來探望她。三年前她嫁給了一個台灣叔叔，但新婚不久叔叔就被調職到中國去……她沒有跟他去因為她不喜歡中國。她經常都是很快樂的……除了跟叔叔講電話的時候，她每一次都是問他同樣的幾個問題：有沒有喝醉？有沒有經常去玩？有沒有亂花錢？……哈，如果我是叔叔我一定說：「哪有！」……他一定有。笨女人。

lots again? Ha, if I were him, I would say "Of course not." Obviously, he is doing it all. Stupid woman.

Boy: She's your…

Girl: My mum.

Girl: She has been busy this week, so I wander about on my own every day from morning until late afternoon. In the evening, I meet up with her and her friends for dinner. She loves introducing me to people here. Last night at dinner, the man opposite, when he was not eating, he was leering at me. I thought, "Huh! That greasy old man definitely likes my mum so wants to be my friend. *(In Cantonese)* You wish!" *(In Mandarin)* When we ate dessert, he pulled out a charm and said, "This will keep you safe. It'll protect you when I'm not around. Do keep it in your wallet." I glanced at that woman, then I accepted it, taking a slow, deep breath, "Thank you, godfather. But I am a Christian." I knew that would cause an awkward silence, so I made the point of saying it out loud. Because that woman, sitting next to my godfather – my mum – had been avoiding my glare.

He listens.

Girl: What really annoys me… when she is with her friends, she never admits that I am her daughter. I am only her niece. She makes me call her by her English name. Doris. And she calls me Maureen. *(In Cantonese)* Ha, then I guess I should call my dad Robert!

Silence.

Girl: *(Continues in Cantonese)* Why on earth would I need a godfather? I've got a father at home. He's my real dad, not a fake one.

Silence.

少男：　　她是你的……

少女：　　我媽。

少女：　　這個星期她都在忙，每天早上到下午都是我一個人到處逛，晚上就跟她和她的朋友一起吃晚飯。她就是最愛幫我在台灣建立人際關係。昨天晚上吃飯的時候，坐在我對面的一位叔叔就不是在吃飯，他那雙眼就是笑瞇瞇的看着我。我想：哼！這一個歐吉桑根本就是看上我媽！想要跟我 Friend？（廣東話）你就想喇！到了吃甜品的時候，那叔叔拿出一個平安符，説：「這一道符是保佑你平平安安，當乾爹不在你身邊的時候，它會保護你的。你把它放在皮包裏啊。」我立刻瞄一瞄那女人，然後我把那平安符收下來，慢慢地、深呼吸了一下：「謝謝你，乾爹，但我是 Christian。」我知道我一説出口一定會冷場，但是我就是要説出來，因為坐在我乾爹旁邊的女人 — 我媽，一直在逃避我的眼神。

【少男聆聽着】

少女：　　讓我最不滿的就是……她在她的朋友面前，從來不認我是她的女兒。我，只是她的姪女。她要我叫她的英文名字Doris，而她叫我Maureen。（廣東話）哈， 咁我應該叫我爸做Robert！

【靜默】

少女：　　（廣東話）我要個契爺做咩？！我有個爸爸喺香港，真係我老豆，唔係「契」架！

【靜默】

The BOY walks off.

Silence.

He returns with a coffee.

Boy: My treat.

Girl: I do not drink coffee.

Boy: This is cappuccino. It shouldn't be too bitter. Do try it.

Girl: Thank you.

She takes a sip and frowns.

He grins; she smiles back.

Boy: Are you from Hong Kong?

Girl: Yes.

Boy: *(In Cantonese)* Hong Konger.

They laugh.

Silence.

Girl: I am not usually like this … it is just that I do not know her at all.

Boy: Just stay longer, talk more. It will be fine.

Girl: It is not that simple.

Boy: Then try not to make it too complicated. *(In English)* "Live in the moment." *(In Mandarin)* Learnt that in my English class today.

Girl: *(In English)* Live in the moment.

Boy: Live in the moment.

Girl: Live in the moment.

Silence.

【少男離開】

【靜默】

【少男拿着一杯咖啡回來】

少男：　請你喝。

少女：　我不喝咖啡的。

少男：　這是Cappuccino，應該不會太苦，試試看。

少女：　謝謝。

【少女試了一口之後皺眉頭】

【少男微笑着；少女也笑起來】

少男：　你是香港人。

少女：　是的。

少男：　（廣東話）香港人。

【二人笑着】

【靜默】

少女：　我平常不是這樣子的……只是我跟她不熟。

少男：　多住幾天、多聊一下就沒問題啦。

少女：　不是那麼容易的。

少男：　那就別想得太複雜，「Live in the moment」，今天上
　　　　英文課學的。

少女：　Live in the moment。

少男：　活在當下。

少女：　活在當下。

【靜默】

Girl:	The problems of the moment, solve them in the moment.
Boy:	The problems of the moment, solve them in the moment.
Girl:	What are your problems of the moment then?
Boy:	English exam retake.
Girl:	How will you solve that?
Boy:	*(In Cantonese)* Go home now, and work really hard.
	They chuckle.
Girl:	How come you speak Cantonese?
Boy:	How come you speak Mandarin?
Girl:	*Meteor Garden.*
Boy:	Sandra Ng.
	They giggle.
	Silence.
Girl:	I must go now. Thank you for the coffee. Thank you.
Boy:	*(In Cantonese)* My pleasure. *(In Mandarin)* Where are you going?
Girl:	Tamsui. I am getting the MRT.
Boy:	I'm going to Beitou. *(Packs up)* Is it all right if I come with you?
Girl:	OK.
	They leave together.

少女：　當下的問題，當下去解決。

少男：　當下的問題，當下去解決。

少女：　那你當下有什麼問題？

少男：　補考英文。

少女：　當下要怎麼解決？

少男：　（廣東話）而家返屋企俾心機！

　　　　【二人笑着】

少女：　為什麼你會說廣東話？

少男：　為什麼你會說普通話？

少女：　《流星花園》。

少男：　吳君如。

　　　　【二人笑着】

　　　　【靜默】

少女：　我要走了，謝謝你的咖啡。謝謝你。

少男：　（廣東話）唔駛客氣。（普通話）你要去哪？

少女：　淡水，坐捷運。

少男：　我去北投，（收拾他的手提電腦）跟你一起坐捷運，可以嗎？

少女：　嗯！

　　　　【他們一同離開】

Scene

香港中環的一個公園
A park in Central,
Hong Kong

Scene 5   A park in Central, Hong Kong

> *Lights up.*
>
> *The MAN is lying on a wooden bench.*
>
> *The YOUNG WOMAN enters. She is in uniform.*

Young Woman: Out this late?

Man: Aren't you out late as well?

Young Woman: Went shopping. Come here often?

Man: Sometimes.

Young Woman: Picked up your clothes yet?

Man: No.

Young Woman: I can't understand why you won't do it. Give me the money, I'll get them.

Man: Nah, I'll do it.

> *Silence.*

Young Woman: *(Pulls out a small plastic bag from her bag and puts it on the bench)* Got you this. A new compilation. Just came out this year.

> *She is swinging gently on the swing.*

Man: …

Young Woman: I know you're nostalgic. But we've listened to that one at home for years. Time to change.

Man: …

Young Woman: It's a bargain. Double CD for 105 dollars. Even got four live tracks.

第五場　香港中環的一個公園

　　　　　燈亮

　　　　　【男人放軟身子躺在長木椅上】

　　　　　【女子穿着制服入】

女子：　　咁夜嘅？

男人：　　你又咁夜先放？

女子：　　去咗行街咋嘛。你成日落嚟架？

男人：　　一時時。

女子：　　你攞咗套衫未呀？

男人：　　未呀。

女子：　　都唔駛你點解唔攞。你俾錢我一陣去幫你攞喇。

男人：　　唔駛，我會攞。

　　　　　【靜默】

女子：　　（從袋中拿出一個小膠袋，將它放在長椅上）買俾你架，
　　　　　今年出咗隻精選呀。

　　　　　【女子坐在鞦韆上輕輕盪着】

男人：　　……

女子：　　我知你懷舊，不過屋企嗰隻聽咗好多年喇，換咗佢啦。

男人：　　……

女子：　　好抵呀，雙碟價 $105 蚊，仲有四隻係 Live。

Man:	You've listened to the whole thing?
Young Woman:	Yeah, haven't got anything better to do.

Silence.

Young Woman:	I know what that squealing man is on about.

Silence.

She sighs.

Man:	…
Young Woman:	I'll probably get fired soon.
Man:	…
Young Woman:	Actually I don't really like the job. One day they'll tell you to come in for more hours, the next they'll tell you to stay at home. Hey, I am human too. I also need to make money. I also need to support myself.

He sits up.

Young Woman:	What's the point of paying lots an hour, there's hardly any work…
Man:	…
Young Woman:	Better get myself a new job before I get kicked out.
Man:	How many times have you changed jobs?
Young Woman:	…
Man:	Have you ever been in a job that wasn't temporary?
Young Woman:	No, but I've tried…

男人： 你聽晒成隻碟？

女子： 係呀，冇嘢做呀嘛。

　　　　【靜默】

女子： 我知條假音佬唱乜架。

　　　　【靜默】

女子： 唉！

男人： ……

女子： 我就嚟俾人炒喇。

男人： ……

女子： 其實我都唔鍾意份工，一時就叫人返多幾更，一時就
　　　　叫你唔駛返。喂，我都係人嚟架，我都要搵錢，我都
　　　　要養自己架。

　　　　【男人坐起身】

女子： 時薪高都冇用架，一個月返得咁少……

男人： ……

女子： 都係唔好喇，趁佢未炒我之前，我搵過份……

男人： 你轉過幾多份工？

女子： ……

男人： 你有冇做過一份長嘅？

女子： 冇，但係我有試……

Man:	Can't you be less loud?

She stops chattering and pushes the swing hard. He sits and smokes.

After a while, she jumps down and strides over to him.

Young Woman:	I'm not like you, staying in the same job for years. Aren't you bored? Aren't you bored of being around us, day in day out, for so long? You can walk out just like her, to save yourself the hassle.

He looks at her.

Silence.

She leaves the park.

He continues to smoke.

She comes back to get the CD.

He puts his hand on it.

Man:	I want it.
Young Woman:	I want to listen to it now.
Man:	I can sing it for you.

Silence.

Young Woman:	You?

He nods.

Young Woman:	You … the squealing man?
Man:	*Gimme that night fever, night fever, you know how to show it… haaa!*

Darkness.

男人：　你靜啲好冇。

【女子靜下來，然後起勁地盪鞦韆；男人坐着抽煙】

【良久，女子從鞦韆上跳下來，走向男人】

女子：　我唔似得你！返一份工返足咁多年！你唔覺得悶咩？你對住我哋兩個咁多年你唔悶咩？你可以好似佢咁走咗去，你咪唔駛煩囉！

【男人望着女子】

【靜默】

【女子離開公園】

【男人繼續抽煙】

【女子走回公園，拿 CD】

【男人一手按下 CD 不讓女子拿】

男人：　我要。

女子：　我想而家拎番去聽。

男人：　我唱俾你聽。

【靜默】

女子：　你唱？

【男人點頭】

女子：　你係假音佬？

男人：　*Gimme that night fever, night fever, you know how to show it… haaa!*

燈暗

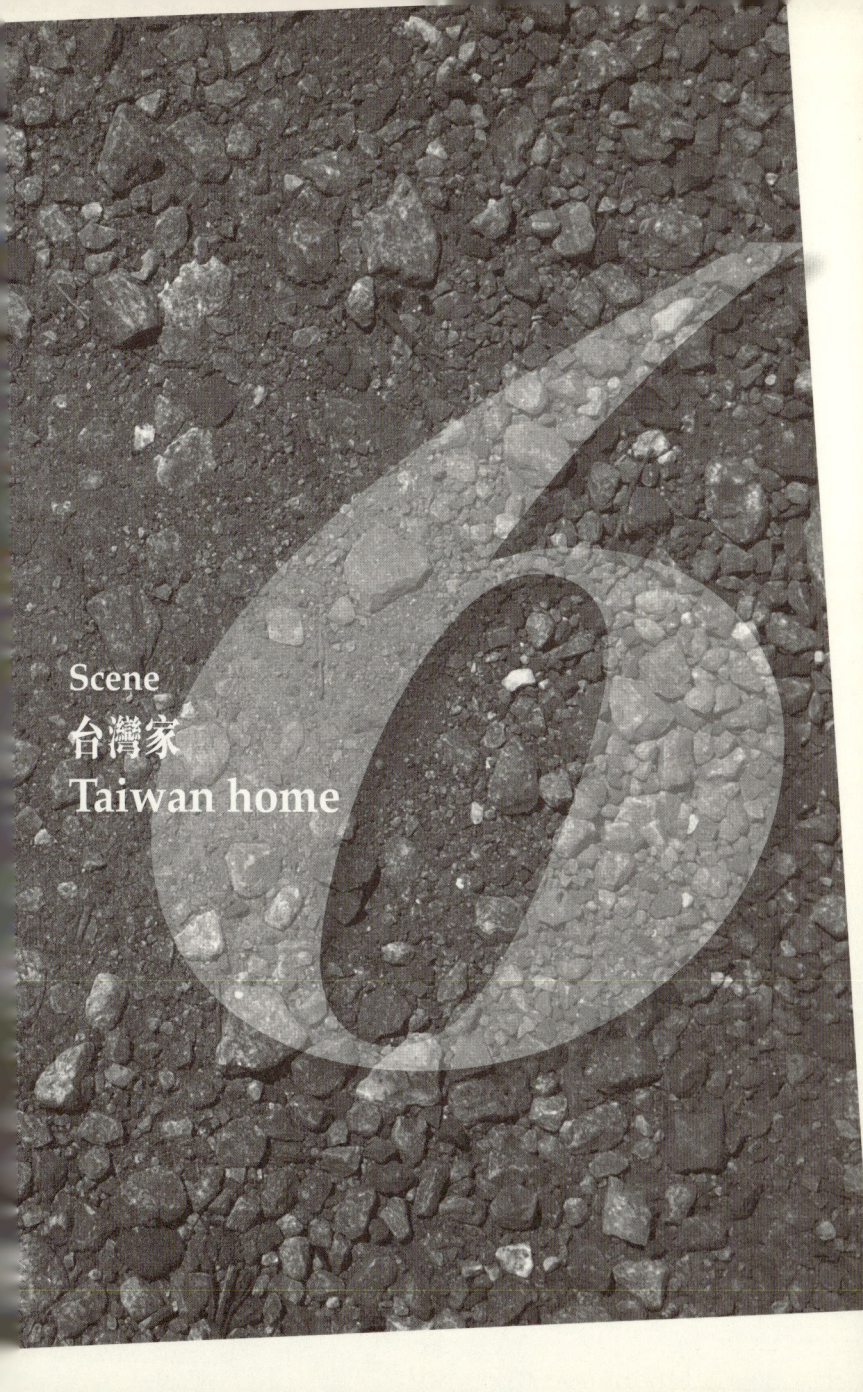

Scene

台灣家

Taiwan home

Scene 6   Taiwan home

Lights up.

The WOMAN is cooking.

The GIRL returns with lots of shopping bags on her shoulders. This is her biggest shopping spree since her arrival.

The WOMAN is stir-frying with her back to the kitchen door. The GIRL stands in the doorway, enjoying the aroma.

Girl: Prawn in tomato sauce!

The WOMAN wipes her forehead and continues to stir.

Girl: Didn't you say you're eating out tonight? Why are you cooking?

The WOMAN turns off the stove and dishes out the prawns. She carefully wipes the side of the plate and puts it on the dining table.

She heads back to the kitchen to prepare the second dish – golden threadfin bream in tomato sauce.

The GIRL watches the WOMAN shuffling between the kitchen and the table.

Lights dim.

Lights up.

The GIRL has taken the camcorder out.

They sit at the opposite end of the table. There are four dishes: prawn in tomato sauce, fish in tomato sauce, garlic choi sum and pork bone soup with carrot and green radish.

They look at each other for a long time.

第六場　台灣家

　　　　　燈亮

　　　　　【女人在廚房煮飯】

　　　　　【少女回來，左右膊頭上掛着一袋袋戰利品，今天是她到台灣以來最大的血拼】

　　　　　【女人背着她在廚房炒餸，少女站在廚房門口聞着】

少女：　　茄汁蝦碌！

　　　　　【女人用手抹了額頭上的汗，繼續拼命地炒】

少女：　　你唔係話今晚出去食咩？點解煮飯嘅？

　　　　　【女人熄火。將蝦碌架上碟，細緻地用布抹碟邊，再將它架上飯桌】

　　　　　【女人回到廚房再煮第二道餸：茄汁煎紅衫魚】

　　　　　【少女看着她，女人不停在廚房與飯桌之間穿梭】

　　　　　燈暗

　　　　　燈亮

　　　　　【DV 機放在少女一旁】

　　　　　【二人已經對坐着，飯桌上有四道餸：茄汁蝦碌、茄汁煎紅衫魚、蒜蓉炒菜心及青紅蘿蔔豬骨湯】

　　　　　【二人對望良久】

Woman:	Do start. It won't be good if it gets cold.
	The GIRL picks a prawn with her chopsticks.
Woman:	Tastes good?
	The GIRL gobbles it down with some rice.
	The WOMAN goes to the kitchen.
Woman:	I call the rice here "fatty rice". 'Cause it's sweeter than the rice in Hong Kong. Having this every day is sure to make you really fat. *(Enters with two glasses and a bottle of Gold Medal Taiwan Beer)* You're so thin. Your face has got no colour. Don't you ever cook at home?
	The GIRL puts more food into her bowl and eats.
Woman:	I've made larger portions for you.
	She pours the beer.
Woman:	Grandma always had a Tsingtao with her meals. You can't get that here. But there's the Gold Medal though. It's as good. *(Raises a glass)* Come on…
	The GIRL raises her glass.
Woman:	Cheers!
	The GIRL takes a sip and returns to the food.
	The WOMAN tastes the food.
Woman:	A bit salty…
Girl:	It's good.
	She eats more.
Woman:	Do you like it here? You can come more often if you want. I'll definitely pick you up next time.
	The GIRL continues to eat.

女人：　快啲食啦，凍晒唔好食！

【少女拿筷子夾了一隻蝦碌，吃着】

女人：　好唔好味？

【少女扒飯】

【女人入廚房】

女人：　我叫台灣啲米做「肥仔米」，因為食落比香港啲米甜，如果每日都食一定會肥死！（拿出兩個杯和一罐台灣啤酒）你呀，瘦到塊臉都黃埋，喺香港好少煮飯呢？

【少女夾完餸之後繼續低頭吃飯】

女人：　我專登煮多啲俾你食。

【女人開啤酒，倒在兩個杯子裏】

女人：　婆婆每餐都要一罐青島，不過呢度冇青島，但係就有台灣啤酒，都好飲架！（拿起杯）嚟吖……

【少女拿起酒杯】

女人：　乾杯！

【少女喝一口然後繼續食飯】

【女人一同吃飯】

女人：　嗯……好似鹹咗啲……

少女：　好食。

【少女繼續低頭扒飯】

女人：　你鍾唔鍾意呢度？你鍾意就多啲過嚟，下次我一定會嚟接你。

【少女繼續扒飯】

Woman: You don't need to feel like you're intruding. I treat it as an investment. So when I'm old, you'll look after me.

The GIRL stops.

Girl: What investment?

Silence.

She throws a chopstick across the table.

Girl: What investment?

She throws her other chopstick.

The WOMAN looks at the GIRL.

Girl: What investment?

The GIRL picks up a prawn head from her bowl and throws it.

Girl: What investment? (*Throws choi sum*) What investment? (*Throws tomato*) What investment? (*Throws but there is nothing in her hand*)

Silence.

The WOMAN nonchalantly picks up a cloth on the table and starts cleaning up.

Girl: Stop acting like nothing's happened!

The WOMAN wipes the tomato sauce from her slipper.

Girl: Stop acting like nothing's happened!

The WOMAN crosses over with the cloth to rub tomato sauce onto the GIRL's lips.

The GIRL and the WOMAN start fighting. The WOMAN sits on the GIRL's stomach, attacking her lips with the cloth. The GIRL twists around and kicks the WOMAN's backside. The WOMAN cries out savagely

女人： 你唔駛唔好意思喎，我當係投資，等我第時老喇，你要照顧番我架。

【少女停低扒飯】

少女： 咩叫投資？

【靜默】

【少女突然將手上的一隻筷子拋向對面】

少女： 咩叫投資？

【少女再將手上的另一隻筷子拋向對面】

【女人望着她】

少女： 咩叫投資？

【少女拋起她碗上的蝦頭】

少女： 咩叫投資（拋菜心）？咩叫投資（拋蕃茄）？咩叫投資呀（拋空氣）！？

【靜默】

【女人施施然拿飯桌上的抹布準備收拾殘局】

少女： 你唔好當冇嘢。

【女人抹掉殘留在她拖鞋上的茄汁】

少女： 你唔好當冇嘢呀！

【女人走向少女，將抹布上的茄汁抹向她的嘴唇】

【雙方開戰：女人坐在少女的肚皮上，用抹布繼續追擊少女的嘴唇，少女推開她的手再來一個鯉魚翻身用後腳肘重挫女人的屁股；女人發出如野獸般的慘叫後將自己整個身體撲向少女；少女用手腳鉗實對方再來一個人肉轉。雙方發出慘叫。疑似打鬥繼續】

and sinks her body weight on to the GIRL. The GIRL tightens her grip and flips on top of the WOMAN. There is much screaming, shouting and tangling of limbs.

Woman: What am I to you?

Girl: And what am I to you?

They struggle.

Woman: What do you want?

Girl: Argh!

Woman: You're young. You don't understand!

Girl: Can't you explain until I do!

They continue to wrestle.

Woman: I am selfish! Is that good enough?

Girl: Then why do you cook for me?

Woman: I'm worried you'd starve.

Girl: I grew up without you ever cooking for me. Did I starve?

Woman: What do you want then?

Girl: Why did you have to bring him when Grandma died?

Woman: He's my husband.

Girl: No.

Woman: Then who is he?

Girl: He does not belong to Hong Kong.

Woman: Fuck off!

The WOMAN pushes the GIRL in the face and untangles herself from the GIRL's grip. She stands up.

女人：　你當我係咩？

少女：　你究竟當我係咩？

　　　　【二人扭結在一起】

女人：　咁你想要啲咩吖？

少女：　呀！

女人：　你仲細，你唔明！

少女：　咁你講到我明囉！

　　　　【二人的身體在拉扯着】

女人：　我自私！得未！

少女：　自私咁你又煮飯俾我食？

女人：　我驚你餓死！

少女：　咁我細個冇你煮飯又唔見我餓死！

女人：　咁你想點吖？

少女：　點解婆婆死果陣你要帶埋叔叔過嚟吖？

女人：　因為佢係我老公！

少女：　唔係！

女人：　唔係咁係咩呀？

少女：　佢唔屬於香港！

女人：　妖！

　　　　【女人一掌推向少女臉頰，另一隻手推開被少女扣着的
　　　　腳，站起身】

Girl: Then why the fuck did you say you're dead?

Woman: What?

Girl: You said you're dead.

Woman: When did I say that?

Girl: You said it on the phone.

Woman: Cause I really am dead.

Girl: Where?

Woman: Hong Kong! Happy now?

          Silence.

          The WOMAN returns to the dining table, and starts to drink and eat.

          The GIRL sits on one end of the sofa with her back to the WOMAN.

Woman: I don't need you to understand.

          Silence.

          The GIRL picks up the camcorder and starts filming the WOMAN, who is eating with her head down.

          Darkness.

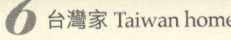

少女：　咁你死乜春啫！

女人：　乜嘢呀？！

少女：　你話你自己死咗！

女人：　我幾時有講過呀！

少女：　你對住個電話講過呀！

女人：　因為我真係死咗！

少女：　喺邊度呀？！

女人：　喺香港！得未！！

【靜默】

【女人然後回到飯桌前喝酒、吃飯】

【少女背着女人坐在Sofa一旁】

女人：　我唔需要你明白我。

【靜默】

【少女拿起 DV 機拍着女人；女人低頭吃飯】

燈暗

Scene
陽明山夜景
Yangmingshan, night

Scene 7 Yangmingshan, night

Lights up.

The BOY and the GIRL each has a bottle of Gold Medal Taiwan Beer. He is talking animatedly while she absorbs the panoramic view of Taipei at night. Behind them stands a motorcycle.

(They converse in Mandarin unless otherwise indicated.)

Boy: Need to improve my English first. Money's an even bigger issue. If I really can study Psychiatry in the States, I'll have to work part time to support myself...

Girl: Work part time...

Boy: Yes, work part time. The cost of living over there is so much higher than Taiwan. I need to save more... but my English is really crap. I've already had two years of intensive tutoring, and I still failed both mock exams...

Girl: Why are you studying English?

Boy: Because I need to pass the exam first...

Girl: Then don't...

Silence.

Boy: How did you like your first motorcycle ride?

Girl: Very much. But I don't like wearing helmet.

Boy: Haha. She's my baby. She keeps me company all the time. It doesn't matter what my moods are like or what sort of circumstances I'm in, she's always quietly at my side. You always seem a little miserable. Maybe you're missing the thing you hold dear.

Girl: Maybe.

第七場　陽明山夜景

燈亮

【少女和少男各自拿着台灣啤酒，少男不停在說，少女遠眺着台北市，他們身後有一輛電單車】

（除特別指明，以下為普通話對話）

少男：　　一定要先學好英文才可以去，更重要的是錢，我想如果真的能去美國讀 Psychiatry 的話，要半工半讀才行……

少女：　　工讀生。

少男：　　對，工讀生。那邊的生活開銷比台灣高很多，現在要多存一點錢才行……但是我的英文超爛，已經讀了兩年保證班，考了兩次模擬考都沒過……

少女：　　為什麼要讀英文？

少男：　　因為我要先考……

少女：　　那就不要去考。

【靜默】

少男：　　第一次坐摩托車覺得怎樣？

少女：　　喜歡。但是我不喜歡戴頭盔。

少男：　　哈哈，她是我的寶貝，她經常都陪着我，任何時候、任何心情都是安靜的在我身邊。你的樣子經常都是苦苦的，可能是你少了一個寶貝。

少女：　　也許吧。

Boy: When I found out I'd failed the second time, I hopped
         onto my bike and left home. No destination, not a
         thought in my head, just drove away. *(In Taiwanese
         Hokkien)* Along the way, I came across an old man
         selling betel nut. I've never done it before, so I got
         some. He had to teach me how to take it. I chewed…
         fuck me, it was disgusting. But he was really
         savouring it. His teeth, all stained red… "Too much
         betel can ruin your teeth," he told me. *(In Mandarin)*
         He also thought nothing is as cool as chewing betel
         and driving at the same time. But the only thought in
         my head was, I've never tasted anything so bitter in
         my life. Though I did want to try it. So, I got back on
         my bike. Once I turned the corner, I spat everything
         out. Really could not handle it any more. I ended
         up at Taoyuan Airport. By that time I could hardly
         move. I sat inside and spaced out. Didn't sleep long
         though. I was worried I'd get a ticket. I rushed out to
         check on my baby… no kidding, a fucking big ticket.
         The most incredible thing was – the betel also went
         missing. That policeman must have been hungry,
         heartless bastard!

         Silence.

Girl: *(In Cantonese)* To be honest, I can't really understand
         what you're saying.

         Silence.

Boy: I can understand you. *(In Cantonese)* Hong Konger.

Girl: And?

Boy: *(In Cantonese)* Go to hell.

Girl: *(Chuckles)* Very accurate. Come on, teach me.

Boy: Fuck!

Girl: Fuck!

少男：　　當我知道第二次模擬考又沒過的時候，我就騎着我的車從我家門口出發，漫無目的地、放空的一直的走。（台語）看到一個賣檳榔的阿公，我就下車去買一包。我從來都沒有吃過檳榔，阿公就教我吃。一咬下去……哇塞！超難吃！但是阿公就很享受的跟我一起吃，牙齒全都染成紅紅的……「不要吃太多，檳榔會吃掉你的牙喔！」……（普通話）他說騎車的時候吃檳榔是最酷的，我心想那是最苦的……但我還是去試一下，上車拐彎之後我就把檳榔吐了，真的受不了！最後寶貝把我帶到桃園機場。我坐在大廳的椅子上發呆。睡了沒多久人就醒了，因為怕被開罰單，所以趕快出去看寶貝……別鬧了，他媽的一大張罰單！最難以置信的是我的一整包檳榔不見了！搞不好是警察肚子餓……他媽的沒良心！

【靜默】

少女：　　（廣東話）我其實唔係好聽得明你講咩。

【靜默】

少男：　　其實我聽得懂你在說什麼。（廣東話）香港人。

少女：　　還有呢？

少男：　　（廣東話）仆街。

少女：　　（笑）很標準。來！你教我一個。

少男：　　幹！

少女：　　幹！

Silence.

Girl: It was my first fight. Fuck, it hurts!

Boy: With… your mum?

Girl: Fuck...!

Silence.

Boy: You two are close!

Girl: Fuck!

Boy: It will be fine when you go back.

Girl: Fuck!
Fuckfuckfuckfuckfuckfuckfuckfuckfuckfuckfuckfuck
fuckfuckfuckfuck...!

Lights dim.

Lights up.

The WOMAN is pacing back and forth outside her building.

The GIRL enters wearing a helmet and sits on the ground. The BOY runs on after her.

Woman: What are you doing? Who are you?

Boy: I'm…

Woman: Go away!

The BOY reaches for the helmet. The WOMAN immediately removes it and throws it at him.

Woman: Go away!!

The WOMAN helps the GIRL upstairs.

The BOY stands on the street, watching.

Darkness.

【靜默】

少女：　我第一次跟人打架，很痛，幹！

少男：　跟⋯⋯你媽？

少女：　幹⋯⋯！

【靜默】

少男：　你們的感情真好！

少女：　幹！

少男：　回去就沒事了。

少女：　幹！幹幹幹幹幹幹幹幹幹幹幹幹幹幹⋯⋯！

　　　　燈暗

　　　　燈亮

【女人在家樓下來回踱步】

【少女出現，她戴着頭盔在地上坐着，少男從後追上】

女人：　你在幹什麼？你是誰？

少男：　我是⋯⋯

女人：　快走！

【少男想要拿頭盔，女人立即從少女頭上把頭盔脫下，
拋向少男】

女人：　快走！！

【女人扶着少女上樓】

【少男站在街上望着她們】

　　　　燈暗

Scene
台灣家
Taiwan home

Scene 8   Taiwan home

Lights up.

The GIRL enters the flat, takes off her backpack and flops face down onto the floor. The WOMAN enters after her.

Woman: Walk. Stop acting drunk… *(The WOMAN turns her over)* Hey!

Silence.

The WOMAN goes to the GIRL's room.

She comes back with a duvet and throws it over the GIRL.

Lights dim.

Lights up.

The WOMAN and the GIRL are sleeping together on the floor. The GIRL wakes. She watches the sleeping WOMAN for a long time, then returns to sleep.

Darkness.

第八場　台灣家

　　　　　　燈亮

　　　　　　【少女入屋，脫下背包便趴在地板上，女人後隨她入
　　　　　　屋】

女人：　　　行啦，你唔好扮醉呀……（女人把她反過來）喂！

　　　　　　【靜默】

　　　　　　【女人入房】

　　　　　　【女人拿出棉被拋向少女身上】

　　　　　　燈暗

　　　　　　燈亮

　　　　　　【少女和女人一同睡在地板上】

　　　　　　【一會，少女醒來，她望着女人良久，然後繼續睡】

　　　　　　燈暗

Scene

香港家

Hong Kong home

Scene 9   Hong Kong home

Lights up.

The creak of a metal gate opening.

The MAN comes home. He is carrying a large bag of clothes which he just picked up from the launderette around the corner.

He notices that there are at least seven similar bags of laundry in the flat. He lets out a guttural groan.

He goes to his room to turn on the CD player. It is The Bee Gees again.

Between bags of laundry, a phone rings. He goes back to the living room.

He looks at the bags, tries to upend one and starts folding away the contents.

After a while, cramps take over one half of his body. It starts as single twitch, then another, and grows into something stronger, more frequent and lasting. An intense pain spreads to his head and neck. He faints.

Darkness.

第九場　香港家

燈亮

【開鐵閘聲】

【男人回家，手抱着一大袋剛從街口洗衣舖拿回來的衣服】

【他看見家中至少有七袋與他手上同樣大小的洗衫袋，他歇斯底里地發出叫聲】

【男人入睡房開 CD 機，依舊是 Bee Gees 的歌】

【洗衫袋與洗衫袋之間的電話響，男人從睡房出】

【男人望着眾洗衫袋，試着把其中一袋衣服倒出來摺】

【一會，男人半邊身和手腳抽搐，最初是一下，然後隔一會又抽搐一下，接着連續抽搐三四下，連帶頸和頭都有疼痛的感覺。最後，男人暈倒】

燈暗

Scene

台灣西門町的一間cafe
A cafe in Ximending, Taiwan

Scene 10   A cafe in Ximending, Taiwan

Lights up.

The BOY and the WOMAN sit around a small round table. On the table are a cup of tea, a cup of coffee and a gift-wrapped box.

(They converse in Mandarin unless otherwise indicated.)

The WOMAN appraises the BOY.

A long silence.

Woman: Why did you ask me here?

Boy: I come here a lot...

               You said you wanted to meet on the phone. And you asked where.

               Silence.

Woman: I don't drink coffee.

Boy: I realised when I got you the tea. I'm sorry. Next time I…

Woman: The other day… Sorry.

Boy: Oh… No worries.

               Silence.

Woman: I worry about her. After all, I don't know her. Nor does she know me.

Boy: …

Woman: Guess how long I have lived in this country.

Boy: Five years.

Woman: *(Smiles)* How did you know?

第十場　台灣西門町一間cafe

燈亮

【少男和女人分坐在小圓枱旁，圓枱上有一杯咖啡、一杯茶和一個有包裝紙包着的長方形盒】

（除特別指明，以下為普通話對話）

【女人望着少男】

【長久靜默】

女人：　幹嘛約我在這裏？

少男：　因為我經常來這裏……只是你在電話裏説要見我，然後你問我可以在什麼地方碰個面。

【靜默】

女人：　我不喝咖啡的。

少男：　剛剛幫你買熱茶的時候我就發現了。不好意思，下一次我……

女人：　那天……不好意思。

少男：　嗯……沒關係。

【靜默】

女人：　我會擔心她的，畢竟我不了解她，她也不了解我。

少男：　……

女人：　猜一下，我在台灣多少年？

少男：　五年。

女人：　（笑）你怎會知道？

Boy: Erm…

Woman: She told you. *(Chuckles)* What is she like?

Boy: Er... she…

Woman: Do you like her?

Boy: Why must it be me?

Woman: Then how come you let her drink so much?

Silence.

Boy: *(Stands up)* If this is about her getting drunk, then I think we should stop here…

Woman: Hang on. Please sit.

Silence.

He sits down.

Woman: Once there was a girl. She didn't know what the future held. She happened to be invited to be her friend's bridesmaid. During the wedding, the best man came over and asked, *(In Cantonese)* "Are you the bridesmaid?" She replied, "What a ridiculous question." Then he asked, "Do you want to be the bride?" She said, "It's none of your business." Of course, it was his business. They got married. Then one day, the bridesmaid felt nauseous. The best man said, Of course, you've given all the best stuff to your belly. She gave birth soon after... The child grew up and grew to love flying.

Silence.

The BOY sips his coffee.

Woman: Could you please do something for me?

Darkness.

少男：　　　是……

女人：　　　是她告訴你的。（笑）她怎樣？

少男：　　　Eh……她……

女人：　　　喜歡她？

少男：　　　為什麼一定是我喜歡她？

女人：　　　那你怎麼讓她喝醉？

【靜默】

少男：　　　（起身）如果是因為她喝醉的事情才找我出來，我想應該到此為止……

女人：　　　等一下，請坐。

【靜默】

【少男坐下】

女人：　　　有一個女生，她不知道將來會怎樣。有一天她去當伴娘，有一個伴郎問她（廣東話）「你係伴娘？」，個伴娘就話：「廢話。」跟住個伴郎再問佢：「想唔想做新娘？」，個伴娘就話：「關你咩事。」……梗係關佢事。之後佢哋結婚。有一日個伴娘作嘔，個伴郎就同佢講：「梗係啦，你俾晒啲好嘢落個肚度。」然之後話咁快個伴娘就生小朋友……最後小朋友大個咗，最鍾意做嘅事就係搭飛機。

【靜默】

【少男喝咖啡】

女人：　　　可以幫我做一件事嗎？

燈暗

Scene
香港家
Hong Kong home

Scene 11   Hong Kong home

Lights up.

The MAN is sitting on the sofa in the living room, surrounded by bags of laundry. A bowl of Kau Kee beef brisket soup noodles is in front of him.

Silence.

The YOUNG WOMAN comes out of her room, picks up the noodles and starts eating on the sofa.

Silence.

She sets down the bowl and goes to the kitchen to get a glass of water. She puts it on the coffee table.

Young
Woman: Take your pills.

He ignores her.

Young
Woman: I've got to go to work soon.

He continues to ignore her.

She takes out a plastic box.

Young
Woman: All sorted out. Three times a day. Four pills a dose. Each compartment is a dose. Take them before meals.

He takes the plastic box, pops open one of the compartments and empties it into this palm.

Young
Woman: Three times a day. You mustn't skip any.

Abruptly, he slams the pills down and goes to the kitchen. He lights a cigarette.

She resumes eating.

Young
Woman: Don't freak me out again.

第十一場　香港家

　　　　　燈亮

　　　　　【男人坐在客廳 Sofa 上，周圍放着洗衫袋，他面前有一碗九記牛腩粉】

　　　　　【靜默】

　　　　　【女子從睡房出，她拿起牛腩粉，坐在 Sofa 吃】

　　　　　【靜默】

　　　　　【女子放下牛腩粉，到廚房斟了一杯水出來，放在茶几上】

女子：　　食藥。

　　　　　【男人不動】

女子：　　我一陣要返工喇。

　　　　　【男子不動】

　　　　　【女子拿出一個膠盒】

女子：　　幫你分好晒，一次一格；一格四粒；每日三次；餐前食。

　　　　　【男人拿起膠盒，打開一格，倒出藥丸】

女子：　　每日都要食三次，唔准唔食。

　　　　　【男人突然放下藥丸，走到廚房抽煙】

　　　　　【女子繼續食粉】

女子：　　你唔好再嚇我。

Silence.

He is smoking hard; she keeps eating.

Young Woman: I'm going for an interview after work today. Hope it leads to something permanent. Make a bit more.

He is inhaling hard and fast.

Young Woman: This is my last one for a while. I'll go on a lighter diet with you. This soup is really greasy.

Silence.

She joins him in the kitchen and takes a filter out of her pocket.

Young Woman: *(Takes his cigarette and fits the filter)* Here, block some of that oily stuff.

She takes another filter out and fits it onto her cigarette.

They smoke.

Silence.

Man: When's she coming back?

Young Woman: Any time now.

Man: No one put the clothes away.

Young Woman: I know. I'll call, tell her to come back and fold the clothes.

Man: Have you ever called her?

Young Woman: Not today.

Man: What about yesterday?

Young Woman: ...

Man: Last week?

【靜默】

【男人抽煙抽得很急；女子繼續食粉】

女子：　我今日放咗工去見工，諗住搵份長工，賺多啲。

【男人繼續抽得很急】

女子：　我食埋呢次牛腩粉都唔食住，陪你一齊食得清淡啲，啲湯多油。

【靜默】

【女子走向男人，她從口袋拿出一個濾嘴】

女子：　（拿起男人的煙，把濾嘴插在煙嘴上）嗱，咁樣食隔油。

【女子從口袋中拿出另一個濾嘴，拿起香煙，將它插在煙嘴上】

【二人一同抽煙】

【靜默】

男人：　佢幾時返？

女子：　差唔多喇。

男人：　屋企啲衫冇人摺。

女子：　係喇，我一陣打電話俾佢叫佢返嚟摺衫。

男人：　你有打電話俾佢咩？

女子：　今日未。

男人：　尋日呢？

女子：　……

男人：　上個星期呢？

Young Woman:	...
Man:	You haven't called at all.
Young Woman:	Why do I have to call? Why can't you call? You only care about her. You never care about me.

Silence.

The MAN takes out a 500-dollar bill from his wallet.

Man:	You don't need to keep me company all the time. Go out more, meet boys.
Young Woman:	*(Takes the cash)* OK.

They continue to smoke.

Young Woman:	I'll pick up your laundry before I head to work.
Man:	No need.
Young Woman:	You can't do it.
Man:	Haven't I got legs?
Young Woman:	It takes hands to carry.
Man:	But you need legs to walk there first.
Young Woman:	You've got problems with your nerves.
Man:	Only you women have got problems.
Young Woman:	Fuck it. *(Stubs out her cigarette)* Do what you want.

She sits back down on the sofa and resumes her meal.

Silence.

Darkness.

女子： ……

男人： 你都冇打。

女子： 我點解要打？你又唔打？你剩係錫佢唔錫我。

【靜默】

【男人從銀包拿出一張五百元】

男人： 唔駛成日陪我，得閒出去拍吓拖啦。

女子： （收下五百元）嗯。

【二人繼續抽煙】

女子： 我一陣落樓下幫你攞埋套衫我先返工。

男人： 唔駛。

女子： 你攞到咩？

男人： 我冇腳咩？

女子： 要用手攞架！

男人： 咁都要用腳行先！

女子： 你啲神經唔方便呀。

男人： 你啲女人先有唔方便。

女子： 妖。（熄煙）你鍾意啦吓。

【女子回 Sofa 食牛腩粉】

【靜默】

燈暗

Scene

台灣淡水
Tamsui, Taiwan

12

Scene 12   Tamsui, Taiwan

Lights up.

The sky is tainted yellow and orange by the sunset. The GIRL and the WOMAN are sitting on a bench, gazing out to the lake. A glass of aiyu jelly is by them.

Silence.

Girl: What did you make me that day with the blender?

Woman: Green apple, green bell pepper, celery, bitter gourd, cucumber.

Girl: Huh?

Woman: It's cleansing.

Silence.

Girl: Have you ever smoked?

Woman: No, but I used to be around smokers all the time. You?

Girl: No, but both of them do.

Woman: Even her?

Girl: Yes, she started very young.

Silence.

Girl: I really like burning their cigarettes.

Woman: Why?

Girl: *(Laughs)* So they'll smoke less.

Girl: I thought of smoking. They seem to have gone to another place whenever they do it. I really wanted to join them. But in the end, I never did. Now when they light up, I turn the ventilation fan on.

Silence.

第十二場　台灣淡水

　　燈亮

　　【橙黃色的黃昏，少女和女人分坐在長椅上，長椅上有
　　一杯愛玉冰。DV 機放在少女旁邊。二人望出湖面】

　　【靜默】

少女：　你嗰次榨俾我嗰杯嘢係咩嚟架？

女人：　青蘋果、青椒、西芹、苦瓜、黃瓜。

少女：　吓？！

女人：　降脂纖腸。

　　【靜默】

少女：　你有冇食過煙？

女人：　冇，但我以前成日都聞到。你呢？

少女：　我唔食，但係佢哋兩個都食。

女人：　連佢都食？

少女：　食，佢好細個開始食。

　　【靜默】

少女：　我好鍾意攞佢哋啲煙嚟燒。

女人：　點解？

少女：　（笑）等佢哋食少啲。

少女：　我有諗過食。我見佢哋食煙嗰陣好似去咗另一個地方，
　　　　我都好想同佢哋一齊去呢個地方，不過最尾我冇去到。
　　　　而家佢哋食煙，我會去開抽氣扇。

　　【靜默】

Woman:	Why did you come on your own?
Girl:	'Cause I'm the only one who wants to be here.
Woman:	What about her?
Girl:	He'd be really bored if we both came and left him behind.
	Silence.
Girl:	What was I like when I was born?
Woman:	You freaked your sister out. She cried.
Girl:	Huh?!
Woman:	She thought all babies are born fat and cute. Smooth white skin like herself. Of course that's never true... You were really skinny, dark, a head full of curls, just like a monkey...
Girl:	Did you take photos? I've never seen any.
Woman:	We didn't.
	Silence.
Girl:	He told his friends that it's really boring being with me. Got me thinking if I am actually that boring... I guess I am. I can't tell jokes. He says he likes to play basketball, so I go along and play with him. He says he wants to watch a film, I go along too and watch whatever he wants. Is that boring? Maybe I don't dress girly enough. I don't like it when we're eating together or when we're talking, he'd whip his phone out to check whatever. It's like he's saying, "You're boring. You're boring. Being with you is really boring." It's all boring, so we split.
Woman:	The most important thing in life is to be happy. Don't brood over something so trivial.
Girl:	Trivial?
Woman:	Really trivial.

女人： 　點解得你一個嚟？

少女： 　因為得我一個想嚟囉。

女人： 　咁佢呢？

少女： 　我哋兩個嚟晒得番佢一個會好悶架。

【靜默】

少女： 　我出世嗰陣時係點架？

女人： 　嚇到你家姐喊囉。

少女： 　吓？！

女人： 　佢以為 BB 一出世就係肥嘟嘟、皮膚白、好似佢自己咁，梗係唔係啦！你嗰陣好瘦、皮膚黑、成頭都係鬈毛，好似隻馬騮仔咁囉……

少女： 　有冇相睇？我從來都冇睇過。

女人： 　冇影。

【靜默】

少女： 　佢同朋友講話同我一齊好悶。咁我就諗我個人係咪真係好悶？其實我個人都幾悶架，又唔識講笑。佢話鍾意打波，我咪同佢一齊打波；佢話鍾意睇嗰套戲，我咪同佢一齊睇嗰套戲，咁算唔算悶？可能我着衫唔夠女仔，我唔鍾意有時食食吓飯或者你同佢講緊嘢嗰陣就攞個電話出嚟睇，咁樣就好似同你講：「你好悶、你好悶同你好悶。」悶就會分開。

女人： 　做人最緊要開心！唔好因為呢啲小事唔開心。

少女： 　小事？

女人： 　好小事。

111

Girl:	So your problems are important?
Woman:	Reasonably so.
Girl:	What are they?
Woman:	I can't remember.
Girl:	How could you not remember?
Woman:	If you don't want to, you don't remember.
Girl:	…
Woman:	One must be able to seek happiness for oneself, so life won't be too painful.
Girl:	Were you really that unhappy with us?
Woman:	No. I never thought it would end up like this.
	Silence.
Girl:	Why did you take me here?
Woman:	I go home. I teach. I hang out in bars. And I come here. And... I come here.
	Silence.
Woman:	I'm going to get a divorce.
	Silence.
	The GIRL sips the aiyu jelly.
Girl:	Don't marry again.
Woman:	Hmm.
Girl:	Men cry too.
	Silence.
	Darkness.

少女： 咁你嗰啲就係大事？

女人： OK 大。

少女： 係點架？

女人： 唔記得喇。

少女： 點會唔記得。

女人： 唔想記就會唔記得。

少女： ……

女人： 一個人要識得為自己尋找快樂，咁樣生活先至唔會太痛苦。

少女： 同我哋一齊真係咁唔開心？

女人： 唔係，係我冇諗過會變成咁。

【靜默】

少女： 點解你會帶我嚟呢度？

女人： 我會返屋企、去教書、落 Bar、同埋嚟呢度、仲有……嚟呢度。

【靜默】

女人： 我會離婚。

【靜默】

【少女飲愛玉冰】

少女： 唔好再結婚。

女人： 嗯。

少女： 男人都會喊。

【靜默】

燈暗

Scene

香港中環的一個舊式露天茶檔
A classic outdoor cafe in
Central, Hong Kong

13

Scene 13   A classic outdoor cafe in Central, Hong Kong

> *The MAN and the BOY sit at opposite ends of a large round table with a packet of cigarettes and a gift-wrapped box on it.*

> *The MAN is drinking black coffee and the BOY is sipping milky tea.*

> *(They converse in English unless otherwise indicated.)*

Man: Thank you.

Boy: You're welcome.

Man: Why are you here?

Boy: To bring the cigarette to you ... just kidding.

Man: It's not funny.

Boy: …

> *Silence.*

Boy: *(In Mandarin)* You're really her…

Man: Speak in English please.

Boy: *(Points to his tea)* It tastes good!

> *Silence.*

Man: How to meet my daughter?

Boy: One day in a cafe… She came in and we started to have a chat – no, she started to talk with me first.

Man: And she ask for you to come to Hong Kong and bring this to me?

Boy: *(In Mandarin)* No, no… *(In English)* No… Ah… Why you keep asking me question? I feel not…

Man: I'm police.

第十三場　香港中環的一個舊式露天茶檔

【男人和少男對坐着，大圓枱上有一包香煙和一個有包裝紙的長方形盒】

【男人喝着齋啡；少男喝着奶茶】

（除特別指明，以下為英語對話）

男人：　　Thank you.

少男：　　You're welcome.

男人：　　Why are you here?

少男：　　To bring the cigarette to you...just kidding.

男人：　　It's not funny.

少男：　　……

【靜默】

少男：　　（普通話）你真的是她的……

男人：　　Speak in English please.

少男：　　（指着奶茶）It tastes good!

【靜默】

男人：　　How to meet my daughter?

少男：　　One day in a cafe...she came in and we started to have a chat, no, she started to talk with me first.

男人：　　And she ask for you to come to HK and bring this to me?

少男：　　（普通話）不是不是 ......No...ah...why you keep asking me question? I feel not...

男人：　　I'm Police.

Silence.

The MAN lights up.

Boy: I got to go now.

Man: Stay.

Silence.

Man: Have you see her mother?

Boy: Yes.

Man: What does she look like?

Boy: Beautiful but a little bit cruel.

The MAN laughs.

Boy: You love her?

Man: …

Boy: *(In Mandarin)* You should've gone to Taiwan with her.

Man: It's none of your business.

The MAN takes a drag.

Silence.

He picks up the box and notices the tear in the wrapping on the bottom. He looks at the BOY.

Boy: *(In Mandarin)* I did not realise. *(Snatches the box)* It's different from what you smoke now.

The MAN smokes. The BOY puts the box back on the table and drinks tea.

Boy: *(In Mandarin)* She just gave me your address and I came over.

Man: You should give this to me by air mail.

【靜默】

【男人抽煙】

少男： I got to go now.

男人： Stay.

【靜默】

男人： Have you see her mother?

少男： Yes.

男人： What does she look like?

少男： Beautiful but a little bit cruel.

【男人笑】

少男： You love her?

男人： ……

少男： （普通話）那你就應該跟她一起去台灣喔！

男人： It's none of your business.

【男人抽煙】

【靜默】

【男人拿起長方形盒，看到底下的花紙穿了一個大洞，他望向少男】

少男： （普通話）我不曉得……（他搶了男人手上的長方形盒）……跟你現在抽的是不一樣。

【男人繼續抽煙；少男放下盒子然後喝奶茶】

少男： （普通話）她只是把你的地址給了我，然後我就來了。

男人： You should give this to me by air mail.

Boy: I want to come here.

Man: Why?

Boy: I want to know this place.

Man: *(In Cantonese)* There's no need. *(Stubs out the cigarette and drinks)*

           Coffee never with milk for me.

           The YOUNG WOMAN enters.

           (They converse in Cantonese unless otherwise indicated.)

Young   What are you doing here?
Woman:

Man: What?

Young   You didn't go to your check up.
Woman:

Man: I've got things to do.

Young   Do what? Say it. What are you doing?
Woman:

           The MAN looks at the BOY. She follows his gaze.

           Silence.

Young   Even if it's got something to do with him, so what?
Woman: You can't miss your check up. He's got his problems.
           You've got yours. And I've got mine. You can't solve
           three problems by piling them together.

           Silence.

Young   Have you sorted it out?
Woman:

           Silence.

Young   Have you sorted it out?
Woman:

少男： I want to come here.

男人： Why?

少男： I want to know this place.

男人： （廣東話）唔需要。（熄煙，喝齋啡）

男人： Coffee never with milk for me.

【女子入】

（除特別指明，以下為廣東話對話）

女子： 你做乜喺度架？！

男人： 咩事？

女子： 你冇去覆診呀。

男人： 我做緊嘢吖嘛。

女子： 做咩？你講，你做緊咩？

【男人望着少男；女子望着少男】

【靜默】

女子： 就算關佢事咁又點？你係唔可以唔去覆診架。佢有佢嘅問題、你有你嘅問題、我有我嘅問題，三個問題擺埋一齊係唔能夠解決。

【靜默】

女子： 你哋解決咗未？

【靜默】

女子： 你解決咗未？

Silence.

Young
Woman: Mine has been sorted out today. Someone sorted me out. They even asked at the end if I've got any questions. Ha, got any questions?

She sits down between them.

Silence.

Young
Woman: I really want to go to Lantau. You used to take me all the time.

Silence.

Boy: *(In Mandarin)* I'm staying there.

The MAN and the YOUNG WOMAN look at him.

Young
Woman: Huh?!

Boy: *(In Mandarin)* Youth hostel. The air's fresh and it's affordable.

Young
Woman: Huh?!

Boy: *(In Mandarin)* Maybe... We could go together.

Young
Woman: Huh?!

Silence.

Man: *(In English)* Take care of my daughter but you should keep a distance to her.

Young
Woman: That's a bit excessive.

Man: No, it's not. I'm heading home. *(Exits with the box)*

Darkness.

【靜默】

女子： 我今日都解決咗，俾人解決咗。佢最尾仲要問我有冇問題……哈，有冇問題？

【女子坐在男人與少男中間】

【靜默】

女子： 我好想去大嶼山，你哋以前成日帶我去。

【靜默】

少男： （普通話）我住在那邊。

【二人望着少男】

女子： 吓？！

少男： （普通話）青年旅館。空氣好又划算！

女子： 吓？！

少男： （普通話）或許……我們可以一起去。

女子： 吓？！

【靜默】

男人： Take care of my daughter but you should keep a distance to her.

女子： 唔駛咁呀嘛。

男人： 要，我返上去先。（拿着長方形盒離開）

燈暗

Scene

台北市的一個空地
An open ground in Taipei

Scene 14   An open ground in Taipei

Lights up.

The clearing is fenced off by mesh wire with only one entrance.

Enter the WOMAN and the GIRL.

The sound of a plane flying overhead. The red lights on its wings are flashing.

Girl: Wow!

Woman: *(Shouts)* They fly over every ten minutes.

The GIRL has brought along a large piece of paper and two marker pens. She hands a pen to the WOMAN and flattens the paper on the ground.

Woman: What do I do with this?

Girl: Write something. Or draw.

Woman: Not here.

The GIRL ignores her and writes.

Woman: You can't release them here.

The GIRL continues to write.

Woman: Why?

Girl: Don't ask. Write!

They scribble.

Woman: I'll write some happiness down for you.

Girl: It can't be written.

Woman: All right, I'll draw, then.

Girl: Thanks!

第十四場　台北市的一個空地

　　燈亮

　　【空地四周被鐵絲網包圍着，只得一個出入口】

　　【女人和少女入】

　　【飛機飛過頭頂的聲音，機翼兩旁的紅燈閃着】

少女：　嘩……！

女人：　（大聲）隔十分鐘就有一架飛過架喇！

　　【少女拿着一張大紙和兩支 Marker，將一支筆交給女人，大紙平放在空地上】

女人：　做乜呀？

少女：　寫啲嘢，或者畫啲嘢上去都得架。

女人：　唔得架。

　　【少女沒有理會，開始在紙上寫】

女人：　呢度唔放得架。

　　【少女繼續寫】

女人：　點解呀？

少女：　唔好問，寫啦！

　　【女人和少女一同在寫】

女人：　寫個開心俾你。

少女：　唔係寫架！

女人：　好，咁畫個開心俾你！

少女：　多謝！

Woman:	I'll draw you a hand.
Girl:	Why?
Woman:	You like to suck your fingers.
Girl:	All five fingers?
Woman:	No, just four. See, I didn't draw a thumb.

The GIRL writes and the WOMAN draws.

Girl:	Why did you bring me here?

A second plane passes. They watch.

Woman:	Are you done?
Girl:	Not yet. I want to write more.
Woman:	What are you writing? It's so small, who the hell can read that?
Girl:	Don't look.

Silence.

The GIRL continues to write and the WOMAN draws.

Woman:	Let's use the other side. *(Flips the paper over)*
Girl:	Oh, what did you say just now about bringing me here?

Silence.

The GIRL keeps writing, but the WOMAN has stopped.

After a moment, she resumes.

Woman:	Hey, we can't do it here. Why are you still writing?
Girl:	It's OK. We can.
Woman:	You'll get arrested and locked up in jail.
Girl:	Worth it!

女人： 畫隻手俾你！

少女： 點解呀？

女人： 你最鍾意嘅手指！

少女： 啜晒五隻咁多？

女人： 唔係，係四隻。你睇，我冇畫到手指公！

【少女繼續寫；女人繼續畫】

少女： 你點解帶我嚟呢度嘅？

【第二架飛機飛過，二人望着飛機】

女人： 你寫完未呀？

少女： 未呀，我要寫多陣先。

女人： 寫咩呀？咁細隻搵鬼睇咩。

少女： 唔准睇！

【靜默】

【少女繼續寫；女人繼續畫】

女人： 寫埋呢邊吖。（女人翻畫紙）

少女： 嗯，你頭先話你點解帶我嚟呢度話？

【靜默】

【少女繼續寫，女人沒有繼續畫】

【一會，女人重新在畫紙上畫】

女人： 喂，放唔到架，點解你要繼續寫啫？

少女： 得架啦，實放到！

女人： 差佬拉你架，坐監㗎。

少女： 值呀！

Silence.

Girl: Why did you draw then?

Woman: *(Chuckles)* 'Cause no one would know it's me.

          They laugh, they write and they draw.

Girl: Let's swap.

          They exchange pens.

Girl: Now you write and I draw. *(Starts drawing)*

          *The WOMAN writes three words on the paper –
          'courage', 'hope' and 'happiness'.*

Woman: Daughter?

          The GIRL looks at the paper.

Girl: 'Courage', 'hope', 'happiness'.

          They release the Kongming lantern in a special way.

          Darkness.

【靜默】

少女： 咁你又點解畫呢？

女人： （笑）畫咗都冇人知係我畫架。

【二人笑着寫、笑着畫】

少女： 交換筆吖。

【二人交換筆】

少女： 而家你寫我畫。（在紙上畫）

【女人在紙上寫了三個詞語：勇氣、希望、快樂】

女人： 囡。

【少女望着畫紙】

少女： 勇氣、希望、快樂。

【二人用特別的方法放孔明燈】

燈暗

Scene

離島船上
On the ferry

Scene 15   On the ferry

The YOUNG WOMAN is sitting and the BOY is lying on the ferry's deck.

(They converse in Mandarin.)

Boy:
(Traditional Amis song)
(Sings) Naluwan naluwan a i yo in i yo in hoi yan
Naluwan naluwan a i yo in i yo in hoi yan
Hoi ya na i yo in yo ho hai yan
Hoi ya na i yo in ho i yan
I ya yan ho i ya na i yo in ho i yan

Silence.

Young Woman:
That is lovely.

Boy:
Do you want to learn?

She shakes her head.

Young Woman:
What does it mean?

Boy:
Welcome to my home.

Silence.

Boy:
(Sings) Naluwan naluwan a i yo in i yo in hoi yan
Naluwan naluwan a i yo in i yo in hoi yan
Hoi ya na i yo in yo ho hai yan
Hoi ya na i yo in ho i yan
I ya yan ho i ya na i yo in ho i yan
Naluwan hai yan a naluwan hai yan
Ho i ya na i yo in ye ho hai yan
Ho i ya na i yo in ho i yan
I ye yan ho i ya na i yo in ho i yan

He sings and she hums along.

Darkness.

第十五場　離島船上

【女子坐在椅子上；少男攤在甲板上】

（以下為普通話對話）

少男：　《阿美族傳統歌謠》
（唱）*Naluwan naluwan a i yo in i yo in hoi yan*
Naluwan naluwan a i yo in i yo in hoi yan
Hoi ya na i yo in yo ho hai yan
Hoi ya na i yo in ho i yan
I ya yan ho i ya na i yo in ho i yan

【靜默】

女子：　好聽。

少男：　你要學嗎？

【女子搖頭】

女子：　有什麼意思？

少男：　歡迎你到我家。

【靜默】

少男：　（唱）*Naluwan naluwan a i yo in i yo in hoi yan*
Naluwan naluwan a i yo in i yo in hoi yan
Hoi ya na i yo in yo ho hai yan
Hoi ya na i yo in ho i yan
I ya yan ho i ya na i yo in ho i yan
Naluwan hai yan a naluwan hai yan
Ho i ya na i yo in ye ho hai yan
Ho i ya na i yo in ho i yan
I ye yan ho i ya na i yo in ho i yan

【少男唱着，女子哼着】

燈暗

Scene

香港家

Hong Kong home

16

Scene 16   Hong Kong home

The MAN is eating a bowl of Kau Kee beef brisket soup noodles on the sofa.

The GIRL enters the flat. She is wearing her backpack, plus a carrier bag and a paper bag in each of her hands.

Girl: I'm back.

Man: This flat is a mess.

Girl: I'll tidy up later. How've you been? Got you some cigarettes.

Man: Don't want them.

The GIRL sits down on the sofa.

Girl: What's this tantrum all about?

Man: I'm not well and no one looks after me.

Girl: My sister's around.

Man: But I've always had two daughters.

Girl: Yes, now you've got two again... I want some. *(Helps herself to the noodles)*

Man: You only care about food.

Man /Girl: Fatty!

The YOUNG WOMAN comes out of her room.

Young Woman: Presents!

Girl: I'm eating. Later!

The MAN goes to the hallway to smoke.

第十六場　香港家

【男人坐在 Sofa 上吃九記牛腩粉】

【少女揹着背包從門口入，她一手拿着手提袋；另一隻手拿着一個紙袋】

少女：　　我返嚟喇。

男人：　　間屋好亂呀。

少女：　　我一陣去執。你點呀？買咗煙俾你。

男人：　　我唔食。

【少女到 Sofa 坐下】

少女：　　做乜扭計先？

男人：　　我病冇人理。

少女：　　有家姐。

男人：　　我不嬲有兩個！

少女：　　係喇，而家咪有兩個囉……我想食呀。（拿了男人的牛腩粉吃）

男人：　　剩係掛住食！

男人
/ 少女：　　肥妹仔！

【女子從睡房出】

女子：　　手信！

少女：　　我食緊嘢呀，一陣先啦！

【男人起身到走廊抽煙】

	The YOUNG WOMAN opens the carrier bag and starts rummaging.
Young Woman:	You bitch, you've bought so much!
Girl:	Got them for both of us.
Young Woman:	Your clothes don't suit me.
Girl:	The street markets there all have lovely clothes. Lots of choices. Made in Korea, not made in China.
Young Woman:	It's all the same. The point is whether they look good on the body. *(Takes out the camcorder)* Was it fun?
Girl:	Yes.
Young Woman:	The boy was here.
Girl:	What?
Young Woman:	Taiwanese boy. *(Turns on the camcorder)*
Girl:	Huh?! You must be joking.
Young Woman:	It's true, it's true... Didn't you send him here?
Girl:	No. *(Resumes eating)*

A long silence.

The MAN comes back and sits on the sofa. The YOUNG WOMAN takes the camcorder with her to the hallway so she can smoke while she watches.

She fast forwards through the footage of the GIRL's trip. One sequence catches her eye, the cigarette dangles from her lips.

The GIRL points to the paper bag.

【女子翻開少女的手提袋】

女子： 咦衰人，買咁多嘢。

少女： 買番嚟一齊用咋嘛。

女子： 你啲衫都唔啱我着。

少女： 嗰邊地攤啲衫好靚架，又多款，Made in Korea 唔係 Made in China 架。

女子： 咪一樣，最緊要着得靚！（她拿出 DV 機）好唔好玩先？

少女： 好呀。

女子： 台男嚟過呀。

少女： 咩台南呀？

女子： 台灣男仔呀。（開 DV 機）

少女： 吓？！講笑咩。

女子： 係呀係呀……唔係你叫？

少女： 唔係。（繼續食粉）

【長久靜默】

【男人回 Sofa 坐下，女子拿着 DV 機走到走廊，邊看邊食煙】

【一堆少女去旅行的生活片段，她一邊抽煙一邊看着，直至看到一個畫面，煙抽不下】

【少女指着紙袋】

Girl: C'mon, eat! Treats from Taiwan.

Man: Are they any good?

Girl: I didn't buy them, but should be OK.

            Silence.

            The MAN picks up a pineapple shortbread.

            The YOUNG WOMAN stubs out her cigarette, puts the camcorder away and sits down on the sofa.

            The GIRL continues to devour the noodles.

            The YOUNG WOMAN unwraps a shortbread and tries it.

            Silence.

Man: You bought the cigarettes?

Girl: Yes.

Man: Good. *(Puts the shortbread back into its box and goes to his room with the cigarettes)*

            The GIRL continues to work through her noodles and the YOUNG WOMAN munches away on the shortbread.

            Darkness.

少女：　食吖，台灣手信。

男人：　好唔好食架？

少女：　唔係我買，但係應該好食。

　　　　【靜默】

　　　　【男人拿起一粒鳳梨酥】

　　　　【女子熄煙，放下 DV 機回到 Sofa 坐下】

　　　　【少女繼續食粉】

　　　　【女子拿了一粒用小紙盒載着的鳳梨酥，打開；吃着】

　　　　【靜默】

男人：　條煙係你買？

少女：　係呀。

男人：　嗯。（將鳳梨酥放回盒上，拿着煙回睡房）

　　　　【少女繼續食粉；女子繼續吃鳳梨酥】

　　　　燈暗

Scene
家
Home

Scene 17   Home

Morning. The living room is very tidy.

The MAN comes home. He goes to the bedroom with some clothes he just picked up from the launderette.

The WOMAN walks from the kitchen into the living room with a glass of five greens juice. She sits on one end of the sofa and drinks.

Moments later, she walks to the window, sits on the wooden cabinet and continues to drink.

Music starts: The Bee Gees, In the Morning

The MAN leaves the bedroom wearing the outfit he just picked up from the launderette. He stands behind the WOMAN and starts smoking.

Darkness.

THE END

第十七場　家

【早上。客廳非常整潔】

【男人從門口入，他拿着一套從洗衣舖拿回來的衣服入睡房】

【女人從廚房拿了一杯五青汁出客廳，然後坐在 Sofa 的一邊喝】

【一會，她走到窗前，坐在窗前的木櫃上，喝着五青汁】

【音樂入：Bee Gees《In the morning》】

【男人（穿了剛從洗衣舖拿回來的衣服）從睡房出，他走到女人後面停下，抽煙】

燈暗

完

The Hong Kong Arts Festival

The Hong Kong Arts Festival, first established in 1972, presents close to 150 performances and events by top international, regional, national and local talent during February and March every year. The eclectic mix of classical and contemporary works cater to an audience of about 120,000 including participants of the Festival's Young Friends Scheme. The Festival also commissions, produces and publishes new works independently or in collaboration with international partners. Festival information is available at www.hk.artsfestval.org.

香港藝術節的資助來自
The Hong Kong Arts Festival is made possible with the funding support of

香港賽馬會慈善信託基金
The Hong Kong Jockey Club Charities Trust

康 樂 及 文 化 事 務 署
Leisure and Cultural Services Department

香港藝術節簡介

香港藝術節成立於 1972 年，為國際藝壇重要的表演藝術節之一。每年均帶來近 150 場由本地、亞洲和世界頂尖藝人及團隊精心製作的表演。藝術節的節目色色俱備，既顧及古典傳統口味，亦具備新穎創意和香港難得一見的表演形式，每屆入場觀眾人次高達 12 萬。近年，藝術節與亞洲區內其他藝術節積極合作，孕育新作，與享譽國際的藝術機構聯合委約全新作品，並支持不同領域的藝術家進行跨區跨媒體的合作。此外，香港藝術節「青少年之友」計劃，致力培養年青人對藝術的興趣，過去 19 年間已有近 11 萬名中學生及大學生參與。經過 39 年的發展，今天的藝術節不論在表演藝人數目、演出水平、節目種類各方面，均為本地藝壇之最。

香港藝術節 www.hk.artsfestival.org

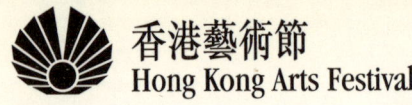

香港藝術節
Hong Kong Arts Festival

贊助人 PATRON
曾蔭權先生 The Honourable
    Donald Tsang Yam-kuen

永遠名譽會長
HONORARY LIFE PRESIDENT
邵逸夫爵士 Sir Run Run Shaw

執行委員會 EXECUTIVE COMMITTEE

主席 Chairman
李業廣先生 Mr Charles Y K Lee,
    GBM GBS JP

副主席 Vice Chairman
許仕仁先生 Mr Rafael S Y Hui,
    GBM GBS JP

義務司庫 Honorary Treasurer
李思權先生 Mr Billy Li

委員 Members
夏佳理先生 The Hon Ronald Arculli, GBS JP
紀大衛教授 Professor David Gwilt, MBE
查懋成先生 Mr Victor Cha
周永健先生 Mr Anthony Chow SBS JP
黃敏華女士 Ms Nikki Ng
李 義法官 The Hon Mr Justice Ribeiro
詹偉理先生 Mr James Riley
黃鳳嫻女士 Ms Gilly Wong
任志剛先生 Mr Joseph Yam, GBM JP

節目委員會 PROGRAMME COMMITTEE

主席 Chairman
許仕仁先生 Mr Rafael S Y Hui, GBM
    GBS JP

副主席 Vice Chairman
紀大衛教授 Professor David Gwilt, MBE

委員 Members
盧景文教授 Professor Lo King-man,
    MBE JP
毛俊輝先生 Mr Fredric Mao, BBS
譚榮邦先生 Mr Tam Wing-pong, SBS JP
姚 珏女士 Ms Jue Yao
伍日照先生 Mr Daniel Ng
羅志力先生 Mr Peter C L Lo
白諾信先生 Mr Giorgio Biancorosso

榮譽節目顧問 Honorary Programme Advisors
高德禮先生 Mr Douglas Gautier
    Dr Peter Hagmann
約瑟·施力先生 Mr Joseph Seelig

財務及管理委員會
FINANCE AND MANAGEMENT
COMMITTEE

主席 Chairman
李思權先生 Mr Billy Li

委員 Member
梁國輝先生 Mr Nelson Leong

發展委員會 DEVELOPMENT COMMITTEE

主席 Chairman
查懋成先生 Mr Victor Cha

副主席 Vice Chairman
梁靳羽珊女士 Mrs Leong Yu-san

委員 Members
杜安娜女士 Mrs Igna Dedeu
白碧儀女士 Ms Deborah Biber
廖碧欣女士 Ms Peggy Liao
黃慧玲女士 Ms Whang Hwee Leng

顧問 ADVISORS
鮑 磊先生 Mr Martin Barrow,
    GBS CBE JP
郭炳江先生 Mr Thomas Kwok, SBS JP
李國寶博士 Dr The Hon David K P Li,
    GBM GBS JP
梁紹榮夫人 Mrs Mona Leong,
    SBS BBS MBE JP

名譽法律顧問 HONORARY SOLICITOR
史蒂文生黃律師事務所
Stevenson, Wang & Co

核數師 AUDITOR
羅兵咸永道會計師樓
PricewaterhouseCoopers

香港藝術節基金會
HONG KONG ARTS FESTIVAL TRUST
主席 Chairman
霍 璽先生 Mr Angus H Forsyth

管理人 Trustees
陳達文先生 Mr Darwin Chen, SBS ISO
梁紹榮夫人 Mrs Mona Leong,
    SBS BBS MBE JP
陳祖澤博士 Dr John C C Chan, GBS JP

網上追蹤香港藝術節 Follow the HKArtsFestival on www.hk.artsfestival.org
地址 Address : 香港灣仔港道道 2 號 12 樓 1205 室 Room 1205, 12th Floor, 2 Harbour Road, Wanchai, Hong Kong
電話 Tel : 2824 3555 傳真 Fax : 2824 3798, 2824 3722 電子郵箱 Email : afgen@hkaf.org
節目查詢 (辦公時間內) Programme Enquiries (during office hours) 2824 2430

職員 Staff

行政總監 Executive Director
何嘉坤　　　　　　Tisa Ho

節目 Programme

節目總監 Programme Director
梁掌瑋　　　　　　Grace Lang

副節目總監 Associate Programme Director
蘇國雲　　　　　　So Kwok-wan

節目經理 Programme Manager
葉健鈴　　　　　　Linda Yip

外展經理 Outreach Manager
梁偉然　　　　　　Ian Leung

助理節目經理 Assistant Programme Manager
汪文鈺　　　　　　Joy Wang

助理製作經理 Assistant Production Manager
蘇雪凌　　　　　　Shirley So

節目主任 Programme Officer
李家穎　　　　　　Becky Lee

市場推廣 Marketing

市場總監 Marketing Director
鄭尚榮　　　　　　Katy Cheng

市場經理 Marketing Managers
周　怡　　　　　　Alexia Chow
梁頌怡　　　　　　Kitty Leung
鍾穎茵　　　　　　Wendy Chung

助理市場經理 (票務)
Assistant Marketing Manager (Ticketing)
梁彩雲　　　　　　Eppie Leung

發展 Development

發展總監 Development Director
余潔儀　　　　　　Flora Yu

發展經理 Development Manager
嚴翠芳　　　　　　Josephine Yim

助理發展經理 Assistant Development Managers
陳艷馨　　　　　　Eunice Chan

會計 Accounts

會計經理 Accounting Manager
陳綺敏　　　　　　Katharine Chan

助理會計經理 Assistant Accounting Manager
曾愛明　　　　　　Ming Jung

會計文員 Accounts Clerk
黃國愛　　　　　　Bonia Wong

行政 Administration

行政秘書 Executive Secretary
陳詠詩　　　　　　Heidi Chan

接待員 / 初級秘書 Receptionist / Junior Secretary
李美娟　　　　　　Virginia Li

辦公室助理 Office Assistant
鄭誠金　　　　　　Tony Cheng

職員（合約）Staff (contract)

節目 Programme

物物流及接待經理 Logistics Manager
金學忠　　　　　　Elvis King

製作經理 Production Manager
廖卓良　　　　　　Liu Cheuk-leung

節目經理 Programme Manager
何玉凝　　　　　　Amy Ho

助理節目經理 Assistant Programme Manager
陳采琦　　　　　　Kathy Chan

項目經理 Project Manager
林慧茵　　　　　　Jess Lam

藝術家統籌及項目經理
Artist Coordination and Project Manager
陳頡妍　　　　　　Vanessa Chan

外展統籌 Outreach Coordinator
陳韻婷　　　　　　Alyson Chan

外展主任 Outreach Officer
蔡樂庭　　　　　　Vanessa Tsoi

外展助理 Outreach Assistant
陳慧晶　　　　　　Ainslee Chan

節目及出版主任
Programme & Publications Officer
曾逸林　　　　　　Zeng Yilin

技術統籌 Technical Coordinator
黎春成　　　　　　Anthony Lai
陳寶瑜　　　　　　Bobo Chan
鄭潔儀　　　　　　Catherine Cheng
陳詠杰　　　　　　Chan Wing-kit
陳佩儀　　　　　　Claudia Chan
何美蓮　　　　　　Meilin Ho

出版 Publication

編輯 Editor
鄺潔冰　　　　　　Cabbie Kwong

英文編輯 English Editor
魏卓華　　　　　　Mikel Echevarría

助理編輯 Assistant Editor
陳楚珊　　　　　　Sharon Chan

市場推廣 Marketing

助理市場經理 Assistant Marketing Manager
陳燕　　　　　　　Lilian Chan

市場主任 Marketing Officer
梁愷樺　　　　　　Anthea Leung

票務主任 Ticketing Officer
關穎思　　　　　　Catherine Kwan

客戶服務主任 Customer Services Officers
劉寶軒　　　　　　Xanthe Lau
楊蘊楹　　　　　　Flora Yeung
姜嘉敏　　　　　　Joyce Keung

發展 Development

發展經理 Development Manager
譚穎敏　　　　　　Myra Tam

督印人 Publisher	何嘉坤 Tisa Ho
主編 Editor	蘇國雲 So Kwok-wan
執行編輯 Executive Editor	鄺潔冰 Cabbie Kwong
助理編輯 Assistant Editor	李宛虹 Lei Yuen-hung
平面設計 排版 Designer	羅美儀 Paula Law
出版 Published by	香港藝術節協會有限公司 Hong Kong Arts Festival Society Limited
印刷 Printer	嘉昱有限公司 Cheer Shine Enterprise Co. Ltd.
版次 Edition	2012 年 2 月初版 1st edition, February 2012
書號 / ISBN	978 988 18176 8 6
定價 / Price	港幣 HK$100
版權垂詢 Copyright Enquiry	香港藝術節協會有限公司 Hong Kong Arts Festival Society Limited

香港灣仔港灣道二號 12 字樓
12/F, 2 Harbour Road, Wan Chai, Hong Kong
電話 Tel : 2824 3555
傳真 Fax : 2824 3798, 2824 3722
網頁 Website : www.hk.artsfestival.org
電郵 Email : afgen@hkaf.org

劇本愛之初體驗版權 © 李穎蕾
Journey to Home © 2012 Santayana Li

出版 Published by: 香港藝術節協會有限公司 Hong Kong Arts Festival Society Limited
承印 Printed by: 嘉昱有限公司 Cheer Shine Enterprise Co. Ltd.
本刊內容，未經許可，不得轉載。Reproduction in whole or in part without written permission is strictly prohibited.